Y0-ABK-619

MAKING THE MOST OF

Single Life

BOBBIE REED

CONCORDIA

Publishing House
St. Louis

Acknowledgments

"Assertive Behavior Chart" from Alberti, Robert E., Ph.D., and Emmons, Michael L., Ph.D., *Your Perfect Right: A Guide to Assertive Behavior* (Third Edition). Copyright © 1978. Impact Publishers, Inc., San Luis Obispo, California. Reprinted by permission of the publisher.

Excerpt from *The Velveteen Rabbit* by Margery Williams, Doubleday and Company, Inc., New York, New York. Copyright © 1958. Used by permission.

The "Social Readjustment Rating Scale" is a reprint from the JOURNAL OF PSYCHOSOMATIC RESEARCH, 11:213—8, by T. H. Holmes and R. H. Rahe. Copyright © 1967, Pergamon Press, Ltd. Used by permission of the author.

Unless otherwise stated, the Scripture quotations in this publication are from the Revised Standard Version of the Bible, copyrighted 1946, 1952, © 1971, 1973 by the Division of Christian Education of the National Council of the Churches of Christ in the U.S.A., and used by permission.

Copyright © 1980 by Concordia Publishing House
3558 South Jefferson Avenue, St. Louis, MO 63118

Printed in the United States of America

All rights reserved. No portion of this book may be reproduced in any form whatsoever, except for brief quotations in reviews, without the written permission of the publisher.

Library of Congress Cataloging in Publication Data

Reed, Bobbie.
    Making the most of single life.

    Bibliography: p.
    1. Single people—Conduct of life.
2. Self-actualization (Psychology)   I. Title.
HQ800.R43   305   80-328
ISBN 0-570-03809-X

5 6 7 8 9 10 11 12 13 14   98 97 96 95 94 93 92 91 90 89

To Merle Demroff, who over the years has been at times a guide, a teacher, a critic, and an affirming supporter, but always a special friend who really cares; and

To Dottie Williams, who embarked on her own adventure of singlehood about the same time as I did. She has been a true friend. One who has watched me grow, given support when needed, and left me the freedom to be who I am, and where I am, and rejoiced with me in my discoveries. I hope I have returned her gifts in kind.

Contents

Single!

How would you describe your life?

"Single and stuck"? Are you defeated by feelings of rejection, fear, loneliness, or past failure? Have you lost confidence in your ability to succeed? Have you therefore stopped experimenting with new ideas, activities, or areas of growth?

Because many people experience common problems with being single in a couples-oriented society, this book deals with gaining victories by . . .

discovering it's your life
breaking free from personal prisons
risking reaching up
leaving loneliness behind
stretching your comfort zones
growing up at last
coping with criticism
managing stress effectively
living a balanced life
forgetting the odds against you

Many people who have integrated the principles discussed in this book have learned that God has not planned a defeated life for us, but rather a maturing process through which we become conformed to the image of Christ. They have learned that our lives are what we *make* them, so the abundant life is not truly experienced by people who just sit back and let things happen! Victorious, growing people get involved in *making* their lives full and rewarding.

I challenge each reader to do more than let life happen:
Make the most of your single life!

1. Discovering It's Your Life

Ernest was sharing with a small group of friends. "I feel as if I've been living in limbo for the last two years, since my divorce. I go to work, do the necessary chores, and things are happening all around me. But I haven't felt a part of them. I haven't felt alive!"

"I've had similar feelings," Connie said, "I've never been married, and I'm doing OK. I mean, my job is fine, my apartment is fine, I have some friends. I attend church and am active in the singles' group. But I often think that *life*—whatever that is—is passing me by!"

Hey, Ernest! Hey, Connie! It's *your* lives! You are in charge! You are making the choices which make your day-to-day existences what they are! Take stock. You too can live the abundant life!

Inventory Your Life

If you sometimes have the feeling that you're not getting from life all that you want, hoped for, or are striving for, then do a personal inventory. Determine just where you are and compare that to where you want to be. Check out your expectations for your life. Are they realistic? If so, then you are in a position to begin moving toward your goals.

Doing a self-assessment every few months is an important part of growing. In this way we know where we've been, how far we've come, and where we're headed. A sample evaluation is provided at the end of this chapter, but you may wish to devise your own.

Moving toward specific objectives frees us from feeling "in limbo" or "passed by," for we have taken control of our lives and are achieving our desires.

Accept the Givens

In every situation there are "givens"—things which are and can't be changed. These we accept and work around. For example:

You are single just now.	You are widowed.
You are a parent.	You have been rejected by someone
You are divorced.	you love.

No given is the end of the world. At the very worst, a given might cause us to take a detour we hadn't planned on. And no situation ever happens in our lives without our being able to profit from it. That's a promise from God.

"We know that in everything God works for good with those who love Him, who are called according to His purpose" (Rom. 8:28).

Even though we make the choices—often very poor ones we realize in retrospect—God uses the consequences of our decisions to give us insights for future choices.

Yvette was trying to teach her sons (ages seven and nine) to evaluate choices and situations, so everytime they were driving in the car they would play a game. Yvette would think of something—owning a motorcyle, for example—and say, "Tell me four good things about it and four bad things about it." At first the boys could only see one side of an issue. In the case of the motorcycle, they could only see good things, but after a little thought and a bit of hinting from mom, they finally mentioned the hazards and disadvantages.

After several weeks the boys could usually express both viewpoints on most issues Yvette mentioned.

How many of us can do that with the negative given in our lives? Try it. List those experiences or situations which give you the most pain. Then write down the negative and the positive side effects of each.

This exercise is not to be used as a scale to evaluate an experience, because the present pain usually seems to outweigh any lessons learned. We often argue that there would have been an easier and painless way for us to have acquired the wisdom gained through some painful experience.

Still, the situations are behind us, and we can't change the past. So we might as well get as much as we can from what has happened. So stack up your winnings and take stock!

When a Given Is Not a Given

One of the biggest problems in dealing with the givens in life is that sometimes we assume that something cannot be changed when it very well can be.

I am reminded of the story of a construction worker I'll call Henry. Henry carried his lunch to work like most of the other men, and at noon he would join the others around a picnic table in the park next to the construction site. Every single day, the scenario was the same.

Henry would open his lunch box, take out a sandwich, and shudder. Then he would complain loudly, "Peanut butter and jelly! I always have peanut butter and jelly. I *hate* peanut butter and jelly." After that he would slowly eat his sandwich with an obvious show of distaste.

Most of the men ignored the little scene because Henry was not a favorite among them. But after several weeks, one of the men spoke up. "Henry," he said, "if you hate peanut butter and jelly so much, why don't you ask your wife to put something else in your lunch?"

"You leave my wife out of this," Henry snapped. "I pack my own lunch!"

How often do we play a similar game? Each of us chooses what goes into our lives. We select our friends, our jobs, our hobbies, our activities, our behaviors, and our responses to events. We can be what we want to be. We can achieve what we want to work toward. Yet too often we simply complain about the situations we are in—when we are the ones who set the situations up. But we are also the ones who have the power to change the situations!

Consider the following statements you may have overheard recently:

"Everyone else in my office is a skier. I feel so left out because I don't know anything about skiing!"

"I really don't want to go to the class party Friday night, but I don't dare stay home."

"I hate baby-sitting. I wish I hadn't agreed to watch my neighbor's children tonight. I always seem to get stuck baby-sitting."

"I come home every night with a headache. The noise level in the machine room where I work is excruciatingly high."

"I'm stuck in my job. I'll never get anywhere because I don't have a college degree!"

In each case the situational choice was up to the speaker. Yet no constructive action was being taken.

Sometimes the situations into which we have placed ourselves have taken years to set up, so breaking free may also take time and effort. But the first step is recognizing that one of the greatest gifts God gave us was the freedom to choose.

But I'm Expected to . . .

One reason we sometimes get ourselves tangled up is that we try to live up to the expectations of others.

1. Society expects us to—
   be law-abiding citizens
   be involved in community events and decisions
   be good neighbors
   take good care of our homes and yards and pets
   raise respectful children
   be self-supporting
   be well educated
   be informed voters

2. Our parents expect us to—
   be a credit to them
   be successful on the job (a socially acceptable job)
   be model parents
   raise perfect children
   carry on family traditions
   stay involved with them
   be mature, independent, "together" persons
   fulfill society's expectations
3. Our children expect us to—
   be perfect (as defined by their terms)
   be understanding, generous, always available
4. Our friends expect us to—
   be available to them
   be loyal, fun, helpful, ready to share possessions, truthful, open
5. Our bosses expect us to—
   be model employees
   put the job first in our priorities
6. Our church leaders expect us to—
   be available to serve in various capacities
   attend all the functions of the church which apply to us
   be members in good standing
   be informed voters on business matters
7. And we expect ourselves to—
   be or do what?
   do everything that others expect of us?
   please people?
   do our own thing and ignore the expectations of others?

The key to being free to live our lives lies in accepting the fact that we are not put on the earth to live up to the expectations of others. Paul says in Gal. 1:10: "Am I now seeking the favor of men, or of God? Or am I trying to please men? If I were still pleasing men, I should not be a servant of Christ." And again, after giving us some relationship guidelines Paul says in Eph. 6:6—8: "Not in the way of eyeservice, as men-pleasers, but as servants of Christ, doing the will of God from the heart, rendering service with a good will as to the Lord and not to men, knowing that whatever good any one does, he will receive the same again from the Lord, whether he is a slave or free." So God has some expectations of us. But they are only those which will help us achieve our highest potential as the individuals He created us to be, so that we will be best able to glorify Him.

What Does God Expect?

Our Father's expectations for us are for our own good rather than for His selfish benefit—as men's expectations are. Let's take a look at God's hopes for us.

1. *That we live one day at a time.* (Prov. 27:1; Matt. 6:28-34; James 4:13-15)

While we are to plan ahead and be prepared to be good stewards of our time on earth, we only have *now* as a certainty. Christ may return at any time to gather His church to Himself. Therefore what we plan to do, we should begin now. We are not to waste time worrying about our future; we are to be active for the Lord each day.

2. *That our lives be full of joy* (Ps. 118:24; Phil. 3:1, 4:4; 1 Thess. 5:16; 1 Peter 1:6, 8; John 16:23-24; 1 John 1:4)

Sounds of laughter float into my study from the children playing outside my window. Happy. Carefree. Intensely energetic. *Now* sounds. I watch in wonder.

Have you laughed today? This week? Just how often do you find yourself laughing out of pure enjoyment of being alive? Sometimes I find myself so busy with an overloaded schedule that the sound of my own laughter is foreign to my ears. Sometimes it seems that too many things are going wrong to be able to just laugh.

What makes the difference in one's ability to see the lighter side of life? I believe the secret is a deep inner confidence that you are going to get through whatever comes as long as you don't take yourself (or the world) too seriously. And it is the knowledge that God is in control.

As the song reminds us—take the time to smell the roses. Do it today! Relax. Take a few deep breaths and become aware of your position in the world.

Look down. There are always those who have greater problems than you do. The less fortunate. The dying. The deserted. The beaten.

Look around you. Others share similar problems and limitations. You are in the midst of a supportive community if you reach out to the right people.

Look up. God is there. He loves you. He cares. He can see the future. He knows how all this is going to come out. Trust Him!

How can we lose? Today is the day that the Lord has made. Let us rejoice and be glad in it.

For today was made for joy!

3. *That we come to be friends with Him* (1 John 1:7; 1 Peter 5:7; James 4:8-10; John 15:9-17; Jer. 9:23-24; 1 Thess. 5:17)

Consider your relationship with God. Do you know Him? Do you consciously try to please God? He wants us to get to know Him. In Jer. 9:23-24 He says, "Let not the wise man glory in his wisdom, let not the mighty man glory in his might, let not the rich man glory in his riches; but let him who glories glory in this, that he understands and knows Me, that I am the Lord who practices steadfast love, justice, and righteousness in the earth; for in these things I delight."

Yes, we can know God. But to get to know people, to understand them, you must talk with them frequently, learning their likes and dislikes, their opinions. We are encouraged to "pray constantly." This requires an attitude of God-awareness at all times. Prayer may be verbal or nonverbal, conscious or unconscious if an attitude of God-awareness is achieved and maintained.

Our attitude toward our friends is supportive and considerate. We do not do things in their presence that offend them. Such should our friendship be with God. As we become more and more conscious of His continual presence, we will stop doing those things that are offensive to Him.

4. *That we obey His commandments* (1 Peter 2:2-3; 2 Tim. 2:15; James 1:22-25; John 15:1-17)

As we spend time in God's Word, communicating with Him, and we become true friends with God, we develop the desire and the ability to follow the guidelines for living which are explained in the Bible. And as we walk in the Spirit, we find that we will not fulfill the natural desires of the flesh (Gal. 5:16). And because God's rules are given to us out of love, our following His guidelines results in a more abundant life.

5. *That we become more and more Christ-like* (Col. 1:9-11; Eph. 3:16-20; Phil. 2:1-7; Romans 12:1-2; Gal. 5:22-23; 2 Tim. 3:16-17; 1 Thess. 2:11-13)

Christ lived on our earth. He experienced the same kinds of pressures as we do. He knew what it was like to have others expect Him to fit different roles. He was kept busy. He was tempted by Satan, even as we are. Yet Christ never forgot to spend time with His Father. And He was obedient even to the cross. Of Christ the Father said, "This is My beloved Son."

13

John tells us how God sees us. "Beloved, we are God's children now; it does not yet appear what we shall be; but we know that when He appears we shall be like Him, for we shall see Him as He is" (1 John 3:2).

Once we begin to fulfill God's expectations for us we will find that we are usually fulfilling our own expectations and that we are in line with any reasonable expectations of others. Coping with unreasonable expectations requires assertive skills.

I Don't Want to Be Pushy!

"I'm not sure I understand this assertiveness concept." Janey admits. "I want to learn to say no sometimes, but I don't want to be pushy!"

Janey's confusion is common. In one of the best resources available on assertion, Robert E. Alberti and Michael L. Emmons outline the differences between assertive, nonassertive, and aggressive behavior (see Fig. 1-1).

Assertive Behavior Chart

NON-ASSERTIVE BEHAVIOR	AGGRESSIVE BEHAVIOR	ASSERTIVE BEHAVIOR
As Actor	*As Actor*	*As Actor*
Self-denying	Self-enhancing at expense of another	Self-enhancing
Inhibited	Expressive	Expressive
Hurt, anxious	Depreciates others	Feels good about self
Allows others to choose for him	Chooses for others	Chooses for self
Does not achieve desired goal	Achieves desired goal by hurting	May achieve desired goal

As Acted Upon	As Acted Upon	As Acted Upon
Guilty or angry	Self-denying	Self-enhancing
Depreciates actor	Hurt, defensive, humiliated	Expressive
Achieves desired goal at actor's expense	Does not achieve desired goal	May achieve desired goal

Fig. 1-1

Learning to be assertive is the process of assuming responsibility for our own ideas, choices, and behaviors. First comes the attitude change. Then the skills involved are learned through practice with supportive friends. Finally the new behaviors are experimented with in the "real world."

People deciding to change a lifetime style of nonassertive or aggressive behavior to an assertive one will want to take an appropriate class at a local community college, if possible. These courses are designed to provide the cognitive input and practice in the kind of safe environment required for lasting behavior changes.

The most important thing to remember—which is the total purpose for learning assertive skills—is that it is your life! You are in charge! So if you are not enjoying the adventure of being single, make some changes in your life!

Your Life

1. Evaluate where you are in your life by using either the assessment tool in this section (Fig. 1-2), or by developing and using one of your own.

Listed below are seven areas of your life. Consider each, then write a list of adjectives in each of the two columns describing where you are now and where you would like to be in relationship to that area of your life.

Area	Where I Am	Where I Want to Be
1. Mentally		
2. Emotionally		
3. Socially		
4. Physically		
5. Spiritually		
6. Relationally intimate friends close friends casual friends acquaintances		
7. How time is spent		

Fig. 1-2

2. List the "givens" in your life. Evaluate each one. Check the ones which are not actually givens and could be eliminated if you chose to do so.
3. Discuss with God, with a close friend, or with a pastor or counselor how you feel about the expectations of others for how you live your life.
4. Read the Scripture texts listed by each of the five things God expects of us. Then consider how you measure up to each one.
5. On a scale of 1-10, how would you rate your assertive skills? If you are under a seven, you might want to take a class. Even if you feel you are a 10, you might enjoy taking a class on assertion, and you might learn some new ideas.
6. Do a Scripture word search on the words "rejoice" and "joy." What does God say to you about this area of your spiritual life?

For Further Reading

Ahlem, Lloyd H. *Do I Have to Be Me?* Glendale, CA: Regal Books, 1973.
Brandt, Henry, and Phil Landrum. *I Want Happiness Now!* Chicago, IL: Zondervan, 1978.

Cordell, Franklin, and Paul Phillips. *Am I OK?* Niles, IL: Argus
    Communications, 1975.
Hart, Archibald D. *Feeling Free.* Old Tappan, NJ: Revell, 1979.
Howe, Leland W. *Taking Charge of Your Life.* Niles, IL: Argus
    Communications, 1977.

2. Breaking Free from Personal Prisons

Do you feel boxed in? Do you feel that you really don't have too many choices about what you do and when you do it? Do you feel that someone or something outside yourself is making decisions about what you must say, to whom you must say it, and how you must behave toward others?

Are you working for a promotion or a college degree that you aren't even sure you want?

Are you a member of so many clubs or athletic leagues (bowling, tennis, golf) that you haven't a free night to just relax and do nothing?

If so, you probably do feel boxed in at times, wishing for a little more freedom. You probably begin many of your sentences with phrases such as "I have to . . ." "I should . . ." "I need to . . ." or "I must . . ."

You are a prisoner.

The world is full of prisoners, only a few of which are in jail. Instead, most prisoners walk around, apparently free to go wherever they wish. They do not seem to be prisoners at all! They go to work. They drive cars. They go out for entertainment. They do whatever they choose! But they are prisoners!

In some ways these prisoners are more restricted than incarcerated lawbreakers, for they feel there is no escape from their private jails. Their prisons are in their minds. Closed minds that refuse to accept new ideas, new concepts, new ways of doing things, new friends. Minds dominated by the past. Never venturing forth, never risking, never succeeding or achieving, never having one grand and glorious moment. Instead, every day is characterized by sameness.

Personal prisons come in a variety of forms.

Fear

There are prisoners of:

fear of rejection	fear of loving
fear of failure	fear of new experiences
fear of succeeding	fear of . . .

18

19

Some people have so many fears that they are completely boxed in on every side. They become immobilized; they can't make any life changes—which means they can't grow and develop as a person.

I once knew a man who was more at home in an office filled with machines than in the living room of the house where he lived.'

Few people felt they knew him well enough to call him a friend because he rarely engaged in social conversation. He was always businesslike, always precisely accurate in his information. No one at the office could recall the last time he made an error on the job. Jokingly they called him "Mr. Computer" because the man was so like a machine.

On the surface Zeke seemed content with his relationship with the world. It served him well. Because he enjoyed his work and excelled in it, he preferred working to standing around with co-workers, exchanging political viewpoints or golf scores. Besides, who had time to play golf? On weekends he usually returned to the office where he could work uninterruptedly. Neither could he discuss best-sellers or recent movies; he neither read novels nor attended movies. And few of his co-workers were interested in the technical journals he read for research.

Zeke attended a large church where he could enter, sit quietly through the sermon, then leave without being stopped by dozens of friendly handshakers.

Each week Zeke followed the same routine:

Sunday—church and reading
Monday—work and correspondence school
Tuesday—work, clean the apartment
Wednesday—work, research
Thursday—work, do washing
Friday—work, grocery shopping
Saturday—work, mow lawn

The schedule had been set up almost 10 years before, and because they were so few, Zeke could remember those rare occasions when he had not followed the routine.

During those years, Zeke had occasionally been invited by a co-worker to come over for a meal or to attend a sports function. He always refused. Zeke didn't spend much time in introspection. He didn't consider himself either happy or unhappy. He simply got up at 6:00 in the morning, worked through the day, and went to bed at 11:30 each night.

Until he was 37.

That year was different somehow. He began to feel lonely, vaguely disquieted, restless. No one thing triggered that feeling, rather a series of events. He finally reached his career goal, vice-president of the company for which he worked. A co-worker, 42, dropped dead of a heart attack. He obtained his master's degree after nine years of night school. There were probably other factors that also caused Zeke to stop and take stock.

During that year he began to change his life-style. He made awkward first attempts at chitchatting with co-workers whose basic response was surprise rather than acceptance. He went to a couple of movies, which he did not enjoy. He tried to read one of the very popular novels, but he never got past page 31. All in all, he was miserably uncomfortable.

Nothing fit. He could no longer retreat into his previous life-style nor fully adopt a new one. It took him eight months to ask a woman to have coffee with him, but the next day she returned the invitation. On their first date they played miniature golf, and if she thought that he seemed too intense as he calculated precise putting angles, she never mentioned it.

Four months later Zeke and Nancy actually spent an evening just talking—Zeke tentatively sharing about himself for the first time in his life.

Looking back over his past, Zeke feels that only now is he beginning to break out of a lifelong prison and starting to live. "I have a lot to learn about living free!" he says with an eager smile.

There are many prisoners of fear. And yet, God has assured us that He has not planned a life of fear for us. He wants us to be free. When we feel fearful, we might break free in one of the following ways:
1. Read the Scripture texts in which God says that we should not fear because—

    We are valuable to Him (Matt. 10:28-31).
    We will inherit His kingdom (Luke 12:27-34).
    We are free (Rom. 8:14-17).
    We are powerful and loved (2 Tim. 1:6-7).
    We are loved (1 John 4:18-19).

2. Make a list of our fears and discuss them in detail with God, a close friend, a pastor or counselor.
3. Decide to take action in an area of our lives in spite of being afraid and regardless of the consequences. (This process is called "stretching" and is discussed in Chapter 5.)

Roles

There are prisoners of roles. Roles that specify the acceptable behaviors, attitudes, feelings, and choices.

the role of parent
the role of boss
the role of worker
the role of a dependent person
the role of an independent person
the role of a child
the role of . . .

When people decide to live their lives by fulfilling roles, they give up their right to be real, for roles dictate behavior. Sometimes society tries to fit people into roles, but often people design their own roles based on self-explanations. These self-developed roles are often impossibly restrictive and uncreative, for they are usually based on ideals rather than reality.

Jon decides that he will be "a perfect friend." In his mind "perfect friends" *always* listen, *never* give advice, *always* share, and *never* argue or disagree. And so in deciding to be "a perfect friend" according to his own, personal definition, Jon puts himself in a role that has no choices. He behaves automatically as the role says he should. And when feelings of resentment or anger surface because of the role restrictions, Jon judges those feelings to be bad and tries to ignore or deny them.

Whether he realizes it or not, Jon is a prisoner—but a prisoner by choice!

When we feel we are prisoners of roles, we may want to take one or more of the following actions:

1. Read the following Scripture passages:

   Gal. 5:1. We are free from the rigidity of the law.
   Eph. 4:15-16. We are to relate honestly to others.
   Gal. 1:10. We are to please God, not men.
   2 Tim. 3:16-17. We are to study Scripture for character qualities to develop, not roles to fit into.
2. Do a Scripture word study to see what God says about our growth and development. Suggested words include:

joy	bitterness
love	anger
freedom	forgiveness
truth	peace

(Hint: Start by looking up these and related words in a good Bible concordance to find the appropriate Scripture verses to read.)

3. Read several books listed in the "For Further Reading" sections of this book. Choose those which sound like they might help free you from a role prison.
4. Discuss our feelings about the roles we are trying to live out with God, a close friend, pastor or counselor.
5. Decide to abandon stereotyped roles (one at a time—all at once is too traumatic) in favor of being just a person in a specific situation.

Habits

There are prisoners of habits.

Aaron, a writer, had just purchased a new typewriter. Thrilled with his new toy, he immediately sat down to type a new article. After completing several pages, he read what he had typed. Something was terribly wrong! At least every 10th word was gibberish! Bitterly disappointed that his prized possession was imperfect, he returned the typewriter to the store, taking along the typed pages as proof that the machine was useless.

The manager called the repairman to the front of the store. With scarcely a glance at the typed evidence, the repairman reached for a repair slip and quietly said, "M-m-m. It's been *malselecting*, huh? You can pick it up in three days, okay?"

Right there, in the middle of a business-machine showroom, Aaron had an insight about his personal life. Only the night before he had been depressed because he seemed unable to develop relationships that worked. He had been divorced twice, and now his latest girlfriend had just left him. Last night's depression and self-doubts had focused on the question, "What am I doing wrong?"

Malselecting the repairman had said in a quiet voice. The word flashed in Aaron's mind with the brilliant intensity of a neon sign. "Malselecting. That's what I've been doing! I've been selecting women whose characteristics are incompatible with my own needs in a relationship!" he thought.

Aaron had always been attracted to self-sufficient, independent, and capable women who had successful careers of their own. He had never verified whether those women also had the other qualities he wanted (tender, affectionate, unselfish). Each had her own circle of friends and personal interests apart from those shared with Aaron. None of the women in his life had been interested enough in building a real marriage to invest her time or herself. The logical end to a conflict between the other aspects of their lives and the marriage was that the relationship was cancelled.

"I've been taking a look at my values and expectations," Aaron said recently. "I still find independent, strong, and capable women exciting. But I've also found that there are other manifestations of these qualities that I hadn't noticed before. I've seen emotional strength in women who are not only surviving but are also conquering experiences from which the traditionally 'strong' women (vocal, forceful, ambitious) would walk away. I've seen capability at the office matched by the ability to be a giving, loving person in a difficult relationship—sometimes both of these in the same person. And an avid interest in some sport, hobby, or career can bring people together instead of pushing them apart if that interest is shared.

"I feel as if I've been given the key to the most complex mystery of my life!" Aaron concluded.

Aaron is breaking his failure cycle!

So many people are prisoners of habits. Often people are tied to a past they refuse to let go or to a relationship they know to be going nowhere. Yet they simply will not decide to walk away.

When a habit is keeping us from moving ahead, we may need to—

1. Define the problem habit in very specific terms.
2. Do a Scripture study to determine what God has to say to us about that habit.
3. Discuss our findings with God, a close friend, a pastor or counselor. (Sometimes extensive professional help is needed when the problem behavior is severe, i.e., drugs, alcoholism, child abuse, prolonged or deep depression, parent-child problems.)
4. Decide on a course of action that will assist us in breaking the habit.
5. Reward ourselves for any progress we make in breaking the habit.
6. Develop a new (and desirable) behavior to replace the discarded habit.

Feelings

"I am an angry person!" Donna says.

"I'm scared of my shadow!" Phil confesses.

"I just never will get over my bitterness toward my ex-husband," Sandy acknowledges.

"I always feel so guilty!" Sally admits.

Prisoners of feelings. First let me say that feelings have no assigned positive or negative values. They are neither good nor bad. They just are. Our feelings tell us how we are responding to situations, whether we are coping or not coping. We do not choose our feelings. We accept them.

What we do choose is how we handle these feelings.

Dr. Frank Freed explains four basic ways people handle their feelings.

1. *Repress them.* Repressed feelings are unexpressed feelings. But feelings that are not expressed verbally, get expressed in other ways (e.g., backaches, stomachaches).
2. *Suppress them.* When we suppress feelings, we fight them. The problem with fighting feelings is that the more we push against a feeling, the more it pushes back! The more strongly we tell ourselves we shouldn't, the more we want to feel what we are fighting.
3. *Express them.* We can express all of our feelings—let them all hang out as the saying goes—whether love, anger, or hostility. Negative emotional expression can be passive or aggressive, and neither is the best way.
4. *Confess them.* What we need to do is confess our feelings. Just say, "That's the way I feel. I accept my feelings." This is the healthiest way to cope with the many emotions we face. Then we decide if our behavior is within God's acceptable standards.

So when we feel in bondage to our feelings, we can—

1. Confess and accept them.
2. Search God's Word for principles to govern our behavior. Places to start include Eph. 4:31-32; Prov. 18:8, 24; Prov. 15:1; Matt. 18:21-22; 1 John 4:7-8; Gal. 5:13; Matt. 6:33; Gal. 6:2; Gal. 5:16; Eph. 5:19-20; John 13:34-35; Phil. 2:3-4; Col. 3:9; Rom. 14:12-13.
3. Discuss our feelings with a close friend, God, a pastor, a counselor.
4. Evaluate how our behavior measures up to God's standards for us and plan to make positive behavior changes as needed.

Schedules

Some of us are imprisoned by schedules.

work schedules
play schedules (Tuesday night bowling, Friday night club meetings, Saturday baseball)
educational schedules
a combination of any of the above

When we schedule our time so closely that in any given week there is scarcely half an hour of free time, and when we live strictly by our schedules, we built a secure prison into which little that is unexpected can intrude. But we also keep ourselves from taking advantage of unanticipated opportunities that arise.

Dave is so structured that breakfast is *exactly* at 6:00 in the morning, lunch is right at noon, and dinner must be served at six in the evening. Other daily routines also have precise times assigned. Whenever his schedule is the least bit off, he experiences a great deal of frustration and has a "bad day."

While we are cautioned to be good stewards of our time, we are not to be prisoners of overly rigid schedules.

When we find that we have overcommitted ourselves and our calendars are running our lives rather than serving as tools for being a good steward of time, we have some options open to us.

1. Recognize that our time belongs to God, and that we are accountable for how we spend it (Eph. 5:15-16; Ps. 31:15; 37:5-8).
2. Recognize that "keeping busy" is often a form of escapism from problems or decisions we don't want to face.
3. Recognize that the human body can only work overtime without time for relaxation for a while and will eventually show signs of stress overload.
4. Make a list of our activities for a normal week or month and evaluate how wisely we are spending our time.
5. Plan a more realistic schedule, allowing for flexibility, free time, and relaxation. (Additional ideas are given in Chapter 9.)

Needs

Often we feel restricted because we are spending all of our time trying to fulfill our needs. We recognize that these needs are legion!

Try this exercise (alone or with a friend) and see if you gain any insights.

Get a piece of paper and a pencil and write "I need . . ." at the top. Then finish the sentence as many different ways as you can, writing as fast as you can. The key is to write everything that comes to your mind. Do not stop to evaluate what you are writing. Try to finish the sentence at least 20—30 times.

Stop and do this now, before you read any further.

The list you have just written may include some of the following words: food, water, love, attention, praise, sleep, comfort, a friend, accomplishment, feelings of self-worth, recognition, a home, new clothes, to lose weight, to have fun.

Now go back to your list and cross off the words "I need" at the top and substitute the words "I want." Then read each of the sentences again, slowly, using the new beginning.

Stop reading and do this now.

How did it feel saying "I want" instead of saying "I need"? Some psychologists tell us that we really only *need* food, water, and air (they can't agree on whether to add sleep and shelter to the list). Anything else we strive for are *wants*.

Obviously, if we get what we want, we feel good, and we enjoy ourselves. But we really don't have to have everything we want. Our lives aren't going to stop, and no great catastrophe will occur if we don't get our wants!

In other words, I want love. If I am loved I feel special and good inside. If I don't get love, it is unfortunate and a little sad. But I will still live, and I am still a worthwhile person.

When we say "I need" we are saying that we have no choice in the matter. When we say "I want" we are saying that we do have a choice. The key is recognizing that we do have choices in our lives. Choices are freedom, and we need not feel so boxed in.

We'll discuss desires next, but first, whenever we find ourselves worrying about how to get our needs met, we can find release by—

1. Remembering what God has promised. He will provide for all of our needs (Phil. 4:19); and His people do not go without the basics (Ps. 37:23-26).
2. Sharing our unmet needs with God, a close friend, a pastor, or a counselor, all of whom can offer assistance or recommendations.
3. Trying to provide for ourselves instead of expending energies worrying about unmet needs. We are to pray, not worry (Phil. 4:6-9).

Desires

Now, about the rest of the things we identified as "needs"—only to discover they are "wants" or desires. Sometimes we become prisoners of our desires. With obsessive compulsion we work toward achieving the *one desire* of our lives:

wealth (i.e., accumulated money, financial security, possessions)
security
health (i.e., physical fitness, perfect food intake)

27

popularity
education (earning one degree after another)
success in a career
fame for some accomplishment

All time, energy, and resources are channeled into achieving one goal. Other areas of life are neglected to the point that our life-styles and personalities fail to be in balance.

The irony is that once we achieve our desires, we often experience an emptiness; we find ourselves asking, "Is this all there is?" Yes. If this is all we have worked for, that's all there is for us. Achievement does not bring happiness or satisfaction; it only brings closure to a struggle to reach a goal. And so, if we are imprisoned by desires, we find ourselves setting new goals as soon as we reach existing goals. But the process becomes cyclic rather than progressive. Even though new and "higher" goals are set, instead of feeling that we are achieving and growing, we feel that we are on a never-ending merry-go-round. We always want more of the same. We aren't satisfied.

So we can become prisoners of our goals. For as we set goals and set out to achieve them, we structure our behavior accordingly. We discard activities that do not assist us in reaching our one big objective. We become single minded.

Consequently, it is vital that we take time to frequently reassess our goals, dreams, or desires to ensure that they are worth the complete investment of our lives. Otherwise we can become prisoners of inappropriate goals. They may run our lives, leaving us no choices. Some goals take years to achieve; so along the way we may discover that the original goal is no longer appropriate for us, and we may want to abandon or modify that goal.

Fran learned this lesson. She wanted to be a people helper. So for years she gathered around her a collection of people with problems. The shy, the obnoxious, the poor dresser, the chronic complainer, the self-centered egomaniacs. And Fran proceeded to "solve their problems" by being their friend, spending time with them, listening to endless discussions, giving them feedback and encouragement. So confident was she that she was being "Little Miss Helpful" that, when problems arose, Fran was right there with pat answers and a dozen solutions.

However, because she was untrained in assisting people in changing life scripts, what happened was predictable. Fran's energies were drained, and since she had few "whole" friends she wasn't replenished. Sometimes she resented having to always "be there" for people who she felt should be learning to stand on their own. And the people she was trying to help were basically encouraged to continue playing out their unprofitable life scripts.

One day Fran gained some insights into the game she had been playing, however unconsciously: "I'll be your friend, if you promise to stay sick!" And Fran began to change. Slowly she learned to stop buying into the games. She became more honest and real with the people in her life. She encouraged people to find their own answers. She became supportive but not the support on which people leaned.

Her goal stayed the same; her methods of achieving it changed. She returned to school for the education and training she needed to become a people helper in the truest sense of the phrase. And, most importantly, she learned to take care of her own life and to build into her social network neat, whole people whose friendships were challenging, nurturing, and fun.

Other people find that not only their behaviors but their actual goals need changing. The variables in our lives change every day. As these variables change, our thoughts, responses, feelings, and habits are also changed. Our needs fluctuate, as do our desires. So clinging to old goals just for the sake of constancy or out of laziness can tie our lives into knots. We become bound with invisible ties that no one else understands. For they're too busy living in their own prisons, bound by their own goals, dreams, and roles, to reach out and untie ours. The knots are inexplicable to others because we knot them with individual designs.

So when we feel boxed in by our wants, we might take time to evaluate our wants in these ways:

1. Review our list of wants and goals.
2. Read the following Scripture passages which give God's principles for our wants:
   Spiritual treasures should be above earthly ones (Matt. 6:19-21)
   Seek God's kingdom first (Matt. 6:28-34)
   Delight in the Lord rather than things (Ps. 37:4-5)
   Make requests in Jesus' name (John 16:23-24)

3. Discuss in detail our want lists with God, a close friend, a pastor, or a counselor.
4. Select those wants which are consistent with God's desires for us and commit them to God for delivery to us in His time. Take time to set appropriate life goals (both long and short term) which we feel would be beneficial in our lives and would glorify Him.
5. Make a commitment to God that we will let go of the desires which are inconsistent with His will for us.

Escaping from the Prisons

In spite of how much they restrict us, our prisons are usually comfortable for us. We know the boundaries. We know what to expect. We don't have to be vulnerable—we are safe within the little walls of our prisons. Life may be dull, but it is predictable.

Therefore, choosing to break out of a personal prison can be traumatic.

There's a movement today that has been growing for the last 10 years; this movement takes the phenomenological approach to life. The phenomenological approach says that a lot of theories, a lot of things have been counted as true, and people understand things in specific ways, but I'm going to start from scratch. Breaking through our prisons requires the same kind of approach, for if we do not rethink our structures and our goals and our plans—the rules or roles we've established for ourselves—an escape is impossible. And when we make it through one barrier, another still exists. Escaping takes more than a desire to be free. It takes systematic replanning and reprograming. It takes choice. It takes being uncomfortable as we begin to break through.

Consider the prisoners in a war camp or prison who spend years tunneling out. They're not comfortable during the tunneling; they're usually working in dark, dingy areas, with very little air and very little light. But they work until they're fatigued to the bone because their goal is freedom. And at the end they are indeed free.

Freedom is not something we can take casually. It does not come easily, especially for someone who has been a prisoner for a very long time. The escape route is there. The growing will be uncomfortable; it may be painful, but it is definitely worthwhile. Think of the people that you admire who seem strong and free. Recognize that they did not get where they are in life too easily. They paid the price. They may serve as your guides. But the tunnel you dig must be your own, for it is out of your own private prison.

This entire book is designed to provide bite-sized concepts which will assist each single person in breaking free from individual prisons and embarking on the greatest challenge of all—being a whole person! For God has not called us to a life of unhappiness or gloom. He has a wonderful plan for each of us!

Your Personal Prison

Take time to evaluate your own life and identify the prison walls you have erected.

1. List the things in your life that restrict you the most.
2. Explain the one area of your life in which you feel completely imprisoned, with no chance for escape.
3. Outline the advantages of staying within this self-made prison.
4. Describe the possible disadvantages of breaking free from this prison.
5. Write a plan (even if you do not use it right now) for removing the prison walls and walking away from this prison by completing the following sentences:

   I could . . .
   I could . . .
   I could . . .

6. Ask God to give you the wisdom to know when it is time to be free from this prison, to give you the courage to risk, and to give you the strength to follow through.

Remember: You can do all things through Christ, who strengthens you. (See Phil. 4:13.)

For Further Reading

Bustanoby, Andre. *But I Don't Want a Divorce.* Chicago, IL: Zondervan, 1978.

Fabisch, Judith. *Not Ready to Walk Alone.* Chicago, IL: Zondervan, 1978.

Krantzler, Mel. *Creative Divorce: A New Opportunity for Personal Growth,* New York, NY: M. Evans & Co., 1973.

LaHaye, Tim. *How to Win Over Depression.* Chicago, IL: Zondervan, 1974.

Smoke, Jim. *Growing Through Divorce.* Irvine, CA: Harvest House Publishers, 1976.

Wanderer, Zev, and Tracy Cabot. *Letting Go: A Twelve Week Personal Action Program to Overcome a Broken Heart.* New York, NY: G.P. Putnam's Sons, 1978.

Wright, Norman. *Living Beyond Worry and Anger.* Irvine, CA: Harvest House Publishers, 1979.

3. Risking Reaching Up

"Frustration is one of the most difficult emotions for me to cope with. I also seem to get frustrated pretty often." Lisa shares. "When I'm frustrated I'm hard to get along with because I'm impatient. Whenever I'm hindered in achieving my goals, I want to take it out on everyone else, and when I don't, I take it out on myself—an upset stomach, a few headaches, or sleeplessness at night as I try to ponder on different ways to do what I really want to do and can't seem to get done. Frustration, I hate it! I guess most people do."

I remember watching children at play, holding little bottles from the dime store and dipping a little round plastic stick into the soapy water to blow multicolored, fragile bubbles through the air. Some of the younger children often tried to catch the bubbles and hold them in their hands. They saw the bubbles, why couldn't they be held? Older children usually knew that one couldn't catch bubbles. But the very young, like my neighbor, two-year-old Jennifer, did not understand the elusiveness of soap bubbles. We had to stop buying soap bubbles for her because every time she tried to catch bubbles and could not hold them, she would sit down and cry bitterly. Frustrated two-year-old!

Other levels of frustration include the level experienced by Jonathan, struggling so hard to copy a neat page of homework, to get every math problem right, or to make a perfect model. He gets so terribly frustrated when he messes up something and erases so hard the paper tears. Or when something on the model doesn't fit, or the glue doesn't hold, and it falls apart. His frustration is usually expressed by outbursts of anger, pouting, and destruction as he breaks the model or tears up the page of homework. He's totally unable to accept the fact that he's not perfect. But perfection is a bubble, like the soap bubble, a dream, something to look for, strive for, observe, but not to attain.

I see so many signs of similar frustration. People searching for elusive dreams, spending their whole lives trying to find such things as total happiness or perfect love. And that includes me. I too search for love. I seem to find it in the strangest ways, when I'm not looking for it. For it seems the harder I pursue, the more difficult it is to be sure that what I want is really there. I think most of us have come to realize that this happiness is not something you ever find; instead it's something that finds

you. We usually find love when we reach out to give it to someone else.

Yet we often keep trying to reach impossible dreams, and we feel frustrated when we end up empty-handed. Sometimes people who've gone to "the top," achieved their dreams, and succeeded in their careers were convinced that when they got there (wherever "there" was for them) they would be happy. And along the way they sacrificed everything: family, friends, relaxation, health, and other interests. All abandoned in search of their dream. Sadly, when they got to the top they found that the money, the fame, the prestige, and the success meant nothing unless there was someone to share it with. But long ago they had cut off all relationships that might have lasted all the way to the top.

Some of us who are still at the bottom don't always understand it when such people kill themselves after finding out that their dreams were empty. And we don't take heed, we don't take the warning, we keep right on pursuing, telling ourselves that things will be different for us when we reach the top. And all along the way we're committing slow suicide by severing relationships and love and enjoyment of the small things that God has given to us. We don't realize that when we get to the top we may already be dead in all but the physical sense if we haven't kept our priorities straight.

Unrealistic Expectations

Ron lost his job as a mechanic in an extensive company layoff during budget cutbacks. After several weeks of enjoying not working, he began to look for a job. Seven months later, when his unemployment benefits ran out, he was still job hunting. His problem was that he was only applying for managerial jobs. He wanted to start at the top! How unrealistic!

Bonnie, an attractive 30-year-old, is seriously looking for a husband. None of the men she dates measures up to what she wants in a spouse. She wants her future husband to be—

between 35 and 42
at least 6'1" tall
attractive (not bald, have green eyes, and dark or graying hair)
single and available
a "morning person"
in excellent health
a "together" person
a homeowner
in the $40,000 a year and up income bracket

34

well-educated
a strong Christian, active in church
physically fit

Is it any wonder that Bonnie is still looking? If she had some way of checking every man who lived within a 50-mile radius of her home (she lives in a city with a population of approximately 50,000) how many candidates do you suppose she would find? Not very many! Besides, those who meet her qualifications for a spouse, have their own set of expectations which she may not meet.

Bonnie is being unrealistic!

At one time or another we all find that we have unrealistic expectations of something or someone. And we end up feeling let down and disappointed. People handle disappointment in various ways. Some refuse to risk again or begin to expect things to go wrong and adopt a negative attitude, so they won't be disappointed anew. Some people keep their perspectives and recognize that disappointment is just something we all experience from time to time. Still other people have the insight to see that their expectations may have been unrealistic, and they take time to reassess their goals. Goals are important in our lives—but they must be carefully selected.

On My Way to Where?

In *Alice in Wonderland,* Alice stops at one point and asks a cat which way she ought to go. The cat answers that it depends on where she is going.

"I don't much care where," Alice says.

"Then it doesn't matter which way you go!" replies the cat.

Setting goals makes a positive impact on our lives in many ways.

1. *It provides direction.* If we have a goal we know what we are working toward. Our activities have been carefully selected to help us achieve our goal, thus some sense of organization is built into our lives. Because working toward goals requires an investment of our time and energies, we can usually work only in two or three major areas of our lives at once. Therefore, even when we have a dozen worthwhile goals, we will want to set priorities and focus on the top two or three at a time.

2. *It provides for a sense of accomplishment.* As we reach our goals we experience a sense of personal achievement which enhances our self-

images. We feel good about ourselves when we accomplish what we set out to do.

3. *It can minimize unrealistic expectations.* In setting goals we must carefully consider what we want to focus our energies on. If we set appropriate goals and then develop practical plans to reach those goals, we are actually planning for success.

Appropriate goals are those which are (a) reachable, (b) measurable, (c) dated, and (d) written.

A *reachable* goal is possible to achieve. (There's nothing wrong with *big dreams* but actual goals should be realistic.) When selecting a goal, we should pick something that is largely within our own control or ability to reach. To become a millionaire in two weeks or to learn German in two days are examples of goals that are not realistically reachable. To be promoted at work within the next year or to take an evening college class in German next semester are examples of goals that are reachable.

Often we set vague goals that cannot be measured, so we have no way of knowing when we have achieved our goal. Therefore, a *measurable* goal must be stated in specific terms. To become a better person (parent, employee, boss, friend) or to control our tempers are examples of nonspecific goals. How would we know when we have reached our goals? We wouldn't! But to read one personal- or spiritual-development book per month and to put into practice one principle from each book or to not blow up in anger for (*a number*) days starting tomorrow morning are examples of specific goals. "Measurable" means specifying how many, how often, how long, how much, or what exactly will be accomplished if the goal is met.

Open-ended goals are almost useless; they must be *dated*. We must set a time frame within which we plan to achieve our goals. The time frame must be reasonable; and it must be one that can be modified if unforeseen variables occur which make the original date impossible to achieve. However, careful consideration must be given to changing completion dates. If they are too easily changed, they become meaningless.

Time frames may be phrased in terms of starting dates for an ongoing goal or completion dates for actions or accomplishments.

The best plans in the world are of little value unless they are implemented. A *written* plan provides a method of accountability for our goals. One of the secrets of successful people is that they live by written personal goals. These are frequently reviewed and, when necessary, modified because of new information or experiences.

Because they do not set deadlines or discipline themselves to follow through, some people have dozens of unfinished and often abandoned projects in their homes. Without written dates for our goals, we tend to procrastinate and often never begin working toward our goals. We waste time. We can even become depressed because we feel there is no basic purpose in our lives.

Following Through

After setting goals, the next most important step to take is developing a plan to follow so we will reach our goals. Breaking a complex or long-range objective into short-range steps makes the project possible. The many alternative ways of reaching the goal should be considered, and the best alternative should be selected to fit our own life-styles.

Sample Goal: Getting a College Degree

Returning to college is a common goal of many people who find themselves single again after several years of marriage. Who needs a college degree? You might! You may wish that you could venture into a new career, earn more money, or fulfill a lifetime dream but maybe all of that seems totally out of your reach because you don't have that magic piece of paper—a diploma!

Why Go to College?

Getting that diploma undeniably requires a lot of time, study, sacrifice, and plain hard work. But it can also be a lot of fun. There is something exciting about learning new ideas and growing as a person by trying out new skills. And that excitement can be contagious among people who are studying and struggling together to master a difficult concept. People who are learning experience the thrill of discovery as they gain new insights into different aspects of their lives. One way for you to share in the fun, excitement, and thrill of learning is to get involved in college classes. There are other reasons to consider going to college.

1. *It is a great way to meet people.* Don't sit home alone and wish you had someone to talk to. Go sign up for an evening or weekend class. Most colleges offer classes in almost any subject you can imagine, from ceramics to needlepoint, from auto mechanics to square dancing, and from tennis to racquetball. What a great way to meet people who are interested in the same things you are! Or to learn a skill or sport you've always wanted to try!

2. *It is something you can do for you.* Taking a college class is a neat way to pay a little attention to you. It sets aside a regular time for you to get

away from the humdrum of everyday routines and to enter a whole new world that satisfies a particular interest. (Unless, of course, you are taking courses that relate to what you do every day.) And when you get that degree, you'll probably feel good about yourself for having reached the goal. You may then be able to get a different job or start a whole new career, if that is what you want.

OK. But I've Got Problems!

Maybe you'd love to go to college, but you feel that it is out of the question for you. You feel you've got a few problems. Some of the obstacles you face may include—

1. *Money.* A college degree does cost money. So you may choose to attend your local community college for several years. The cost is minimal; often no tuition is involved. When you transfer to a four-year college or university, you may want to apply for financial assistance, a scholarship, a student loan (with long-term payback arrangements), or a federal grant. A counselor at your local college should be able to provide you with guidance in making financial arrangements that will allow you to get your degree.
2. *Time.* Most four-year degrees require about 124 semester units. That is at least 2,232 classroom hours, not counting homework and study time!

   But there are some ways to cut this time or to at least make it manageable. Perhaps you have already taken some classes which can apply toward your degree. Maybe you've learned a lot of things on your own (on the job, by watching television, or by reading) which others learn in college. You can usually get college credit for this learning by challenging the course or through the College Level Examination Program (CLEP) which is accepted by most colleges. (For information write CLEP, Box 2815, Princeton, NJ 08540)

   Because many of today's educators are aware of the time constraints most adults face, they have explored new ways to bring education to the people. Many colleges offer television courses on local stations. Students watch the programs, do the homework, and only go to the college to take the midterm and final examinations. (In some states you can take up to 15 units a semester this way!) Other colleges offer courses through the local newspapers. Some offer intensive semesters where students attend six eight-hour sessions on Saturdays or holidays rather than attending a weekly class for an entire semester. Finally, many colleges offer "external degrees" which use a variety of study options instead of the standard classroom program.

Be sure to ask your local college or university about these alternatives when considering going back to school.

3. *No high school diploma.* Most colleges require a high school diploma. However, if you don't have one, then you can take the General Education Diploma (GED) exam which is an acceptable alternative. Again, your local college can direct you to the agency in your area which will give you a pretest to determine what areas (if any) you need to study before taking the actual exam. These agencies often provide classes to prepare you for the exam, if you feel this would help you.

4. *Not a good student.* You may not have been a good student back in some ancient past! Don't let that stop you now. You're in a different place and at a different time of life than you were last year or 10 years ago. Studying may be easier for you now. And if not, then arrange to study with a fellow classmate and take only one or two classes at a time—or even hire a tutor! Why not?

Also, you can take a number of classes for credit/no credit (pass/fail) rather than for a letter grade.

A Few Cautions

Before you dash out and sign up for 15 classes, listen to a few cautions.

Don't just take classes indiscriminately. You can only use a certain number of electives and only a specified number of lower-division classes. Some courses are nontransferable. Some private colleges or adult education courses are not accredited and won't transfer to a four-year college. So be sure to plan your classes carefully. Don't waste your time, effort, and money on the wrong classes.

The Practical Application

Cynthia's goal is a master's degree in psychology. She is 40 years old, a high school graduate and has taken a few college courses over the past several years. Her step-by-step plan looks like this:

This week: To contact the local community college for—
  a. a list of required undergraduate classes
  b. an appointment with an educational counselor (usually takes two weeks)
  c. an application for admission to the college

Next week:	To write for all her high school and college transcripts be sent to the community college
Third week:	To meet with the educational counselor to—

a. discuss opportunities for classes (possible number of existing units; possible challenge of any courses; possible television, newspaper, extension, or evening courses)

b. plan a realistic program of study

Next semester: To start the program of study

Follow through with the plan.

Keeping Our Feet on the Ground

It is fun to daydream wonderful fantasies which are very unlikely to come true. It's necessary to dream impossible dreams sometimes, for in the striving for them we often achieve far more than if we hadn't set our sights so high. But it's best of all to set realistic goals, develop plans, and follow through until we reach our goals.

Your Goals

1. Evaluate how you are spending your goal-directed energies by—
   a. listing everything you are trying to accomplish or expecting to achieve within the next 12 months
   b. Setting priorities by writing a "1" next to the goal you feel to be most important and a "2" beside the next most important goal and so on
   c. identifying how much time you spend in a normal week (or month) working toward each goal.
2. List the goals you would like to build into your life if you had the time or energy.
3. Select two or three goals from the two lists to work on for the next six months.
   a. Write these goals, with completion (or starting) dates.
   b. Consider alternatives for reaching these goals.
   c. Develop a written follow-through plan.
   d. Discuss your goals with God, a close friend, pastor, or counselor.
   e. Keep your plan where you can see it (on the refrigerator, the kitchen cabinet door, the bulletin board).
   f. As you reach a goal, cross it off of your list and celebrate.
   g. Set a new goal to replace each goal you reach.

For Further Reading

Augsburger, David. *The Freedom of Forgiveness.* Chicago, IL: Moody Press, 1973.

Powell, John. *Why Am I Afraid to Love?* Niles, IL: Argus Communications, 1972, 1967.

Powell, John. *Why Am I Afraid to Tell You Who I Am?* Niles, IL: Argus Communications, 1969.

Satir, Virginia. *Self-Esteem: A Declaration.* Millbrae, CA: Celestial Arts, 1975.

Steere, Daniel. *I Am—I Can.* Old Tappan, NJ: Revell, 1973.

4. Leaving Loneliness Behind

Loneliness is one of the major problems for many singles who find it difficult to fend off depression when sitting home alone at night. Because we have all experienced loneliness, it is a familiar topic of discussion during sharing sessions. Recently I attended a small group discussion and listened to some surprisingly honest and insightful responses to the assigned discussion question, which was to complete this sentence: "I ensure my own loneliness by . . ."

Ken started off. "This is really interesting! Only a few weeks ago, sitting in my apartment over the fourth of July weekend, I realized how totally alone I felt. How come everyone at work had exciting plans for the holiday except me? Within a few minutes I was galloping along the road to depression as I began to feel more and more sorry for myself. Idly I wondered just how I'd gotten myself into this situation. How could I be well organized and successful in my career and be such a social failure? Intrigued, I started to list all of the ways I had isolated myself from other people. Soon I realized what an expert wall-builder I had become.

"For example, I rarely took time for coffee breaks with the guys at work because I didn't want to stop what I was working on just because it was 9:15 in the morning. Actually, few people even bothered to invite me to go to break anymore because I so seldom went. I rarely went to lunch with the others at work because they all love hamburgers, French fries, and chocolate malts, and I'm always on a diet. So I brown-bagged it—alone in the office. I'm uncomfortable at parties, so usually I don't go. Or if I went to a party I'd either sit quietly in the corner by the coffee pot, or I'd overdo things and take over by getting everyone organized into a parlor game whether they wanted to participate or not."

"I've been considering the way I relate to people." Rhoda's answer was barely audible. "I rarely compliment people on a job well done or for a good idea because I guess I think they don't really want my opinion anyway. Whenever someone compliments me, I shrug it off with a casual laugh because I don't want to take it seriously in case they don't mean it. Also, when someone introduces themselves to me (other than in a job situation) I'm uncomfortable and respond with my name and then find an

42

excuse to go into the other room or to walk away. I think some changes are in order!"

Max: "I rarely try a new sport or activity. I hate to look silly."

Shelly: "I don't take many risks because I can't stand to fail."

Tim: "My favorite hobbies are things I do alone at home such as reading, watching television, listening to music, and working crossword puzzles."

Ned: "I maintain a busy schedule so I have no time for impromptu invitations. For example, I have volunteered to work a lot of overtime on a special project, signed up for 15 units of college work this semester, and will try to maintain an 'A' average, which means a lot of homework and study."

Peter: "I've kept my telephone number unlisted so no one could look me up in the telephone book and call. I don't invite people over to my house because they probably wouldn't come anyway."

Anne: "Whenever I'm angry I either withdraw and refuse to talk about the issue, or I blow up and say things I later regret."

Milly: "I guess I brag a little too much about my superior abilities on the job. Then I balance the bragging by frequently putting myself down and apologizing for my weaknesses and inabilities. People don't like either approach."

Patty shared thoughtfully. "I guess just often enough to prove to myself that I really didn't need other people, I'd reach out. Of course, to be honest about it, I usually chose the wrong person (someone who really didn't like me), the wrong time (when they were already angry, upset, or hurt), and the wrong way (I'd attack, let them down, or offer 'constructive criticism'). It worked every time. They'd reject me, and I could retreat to my safe, lonely apartment and nod my head sagely. I'd known all along. No one wanted to be my friend."

The circle completed, Ken shared again.

"I discovered that for at least the last five years, I'd lived with two constant fears: (1) That someone would break through all of the barriers I'd built and actually get to know the real, vulnerable me; (2) That no one would!

"Since that day a few weeks ago, when I was painfully honest with myself, I've been tearing down part of the wall that had not only kept people out but had also shut me inside a very lonely world. Just as a mason can use bricks to either build a wall or a bridge, I could choose to either use my behaviors to build walls between myself and others or to build bridges between us. I began to change my behaviors one at a time. I still keep some time for myself, but I am also getting involved with others. Guess what? Sometimes people can be fun! And I feel less lonely!"

Self-Induced

Surprisingly, our loneliness is often self-induced. We fail to build the kind of relationships we need to keep from being lonely. In a recent episode of the popular television series "Mork and Mindy," Mork, the usually crazy, but sometimes surprisingly wise, alien comments on loneliness in a report to his superiors. Mork states that most humans suffer from a common illness—loneliness, which comes from not trusting others. His superior asks, "Why don't humans get together and discover a cure for this loneliness?" Mork replies that if everyone worked together, they wouldn't need a cure!

While getting together isn't the total cure—the first step in surviving or eliminating loneliness is to build some people into our lives!

Where to Meet People

"There are so many people in the world. Why don't we know more of them?" asked a friend of mine last week as we stood in the passenger line at a busy airport. We watched people dashing through the front door, shuffling from foot to foot as they waited in lines, and then scurrying off to find departure gates. Probably many potential friends were passing us by, I thought. But I couldn't very well reach out and grab someone and say, "Hey, I'd like to meet you!" Yet most singles are very interested in meeting other singles who are also exciting, interesting people.

Just how does one build other people into his life? There are two parts to the process: (1) finding the people, and (2) establishing close relationships. First you have to go where the other folks are. Few of us bump into lots of people in our livingrooms! We need to get out and get involved in activities where we are most likely to meet other single people. Have you tried these ideas?

1. Sign up for adult education or evening college classes.
2. Join local clubs. (See your newspaper or telephone book yellow pages for announcements or listings.)
3. Join a bowling league or take up another group sport.
4. Attend the PTA meetings at your child's school.
5. Grocery shop at unusual hours (maybe choose a store next to a 'singles' apartment complex).
6. Do your wash at a different laundromat every few weeks.
7. Phone all of the churches in your area to discover which ones have singles activities. Get their calendars and pick out those functions which interest you. Then go! Don't wait for a formal invitation.

8. Go to the beach or city park for a picnic—alone or with your children.
9. Sign up for personal-growth seminars and meet others who are interested in growing.
10. Take one of those summer or holiday "trips for college credit" offered by your local college.
11. Go to workshops and conferences in other cities.
12. Get a new job, one that puts you in contact with people. (Hint: A woman working in the babywear department of a big store isn't too likely to meet many interesting single men. Transfer to the men's department!)
13. Become an active host or hostess. Begin inviting the members of your singles class (or people from your work, school, or club) to your house for coffee and conversation after the sessions.
14. Work as a volunteer in a local hospital, facility for the handicapped, or home for the aged.
15. Hold an open house and get to know your neighbors.
Above all, be creative. There are millions of people all around us. Get out in the mainstream and meet a few.

The second part of the process, making friends, is more difficult. You no doubt have your own way of reaching out to a stranger, but here are a few ideas you may find helpful.

The first thing to remember is a principle I learned from a salesmanship course.

You have to talk to ten prospects before you make a sale!

Just so with friend making. You may have to talk to 10 people before you find a person you want to be your friend—and who also wants to be friends with you. So when the first nine people you meet turn you off (or are turned off by you) don't get discouraged because you know you're getting close to meeting a super-neat friend.

The next thing to remember is that your first conversation with a potential new friend may not be earthshaking in content. You may merely discuss the weather, what you are doing (waiting for a bus, first time in a new class, etc.). People don't usually open up to strangers and tell all their innermost thoughts and dreams. So learn to ask questions that will get people talking without feeling threatened or embarrassed. And then, of course, listen to what they say when they answer your questions.

Make a point of remembering what people say to you. At a second meeting if you remember that your new friend doesn't drink coffee or takes tea with cream you will show that you were interested enough to pay attention to what was said.

Also be ready to open up to people—but not too much too fast. If you are too eager to make friends, you may fall into the trap of being too open too quickly. People are often uncomfortable when relative strangers tell all about their personal lives, problems, failures, and faults. So try to be as candid as, but no more than, the new relationship warrants.

Another thing to remember when making new friends is not to be too sensitive or easily hurt. You can't expect people who do not actually know you to care for you so much that they will watch everything they say and do so as not to hurt your feelings. Only when deeper friendships develop can you expect others to respect your feelings a little more. If you are too fragile, people will tend to keep away from you. They don't want to hurt you, but they won't want to have to "tiptoe" around you either.

Finally, be a giving person. Give of yourself, your time, your hospitality, your interest, and your love. Give as much of these things as you feel new friendships are worth to you. If you give more than you feel is "fair" you are in danger of resenting those to whom you are giving.

I suppose it all adds up to the old saying: To make friends, be one.

Touch and Go Encounters

One of the risks of meeting new people is finding someone at a gathering (class, conference, workshop) with whom you are very compatible and never seeing them again after that first encounter. Or making a good friend, and then having him or her move on in their personal life and disrupt the closeness of your new intimacy.

A sadness came over Helen as she drove home one day last summer. A close friend, someone whom she had learned to trust and respect had just told her that he was moving on. She was happy for him that he was making a neat choice in his personal growth and was starting out in a new direction which could take him all over the country. It was exciting to share in his plans. However, she would be losing the personal contact that had meant so much to her during the last few years. She felt bereft.

Negative thoughts filled her head. Why bother making friends? she asked herself. They always leave. Today's world is full of temporary relationships. People are always on the move. She liked having neat people in her life, so she kept building them in, and they kept leaving when their life-styles took a different turn from hers. As they left, they took a part of her with them. And afterward, she was never the same. Perhaps if she never made close friends, she'd never have to experience this familiar loss again! Perhaps her life would be free from this pain.

Then she remembered that she also often moved on, leaving others behind. And she had probably left loneliness behind her. Besides, she wouldn't want to miss out on the creative excitement of having great friends. So Helen began to think more positively again.

A few years ago I started growing in the area of accepting and enjoying "touch and go" encounters. Learning to accept these temporary conversations was a big step for someone who had always craved deep friendships. Like most people I have heard stories of people who have lived in the same town for all of their lives and their friendships go back 20 years or more. Doesn't that sound safe and reassuring? Building friendships takes effort and time. When one has invested time and effort in someone's life, it is hard to lose the friendship. So for most of my life I tried to select people who I felt would be around for awhile and then take the time to build a good friendship. I didn't need a lot of close friends, just one or two (that's all I could support because of the amount of time and energy I could spend making the friendship work). So when one or both of those friends would move along and take another direction (taking up a special interest which didn't include me, moving away physically, getting married) I felt the loss more deeply than was beneficial to me.

On the other hand if people came into my life who were obviously just there temporarily, I would be polite and friendly, but I would not take time to get to know them or share myself with them. It wasn't worth the effort, right?

That was my style until about seven or eight years ago. At that time I attended a seminar where the speaker challenged us to take time to enjoy the *now*. Learn to appreciate the sunset which lasts only a moment or two. Learn to have fun with strangers who may come into your life for only an hour or so. Be open and taste the pleasure of the temporary things and times, for when they are gone, they are gone forever and can't be recaptured at your whim.

I considered the challenge. I spent one entire day of the conference enjoying the company of one of the other guests whom I had never met before. We laughed and played. We ate together. We shared ideas and feelings. I told myself that this was just one day out of my life, and it would never be repeated. And I was not to wish that something more would develop. This friendship was temporary. Sure enough, I never saw the man again. But I wasn't able to completely cut off a lifetime habit. Since he had given me his telephone number and address and had invited me to keep in touch, I did. I wrote him a note and called him once or twice after the conference. He was polite and pleasant. But the message was clear: Why didn't I realize that "our day" was over. It had been part of the conference and nothing more. I thought it over and decided that the day had been thoroughly enjoyable and a lot of fun. We hadn't invested very much in each other's lives, but we had shared a day together. I grew a little as I decided to let go.

As we begin to accept each encounter with a new person for what it is, we grow. A lunch. A party. A date. An evening of sharing. Nothing more. Not necessarily the first step on the road to a deep, lasting relationship, but a pleasant experience, complete in itself. Sometimes we succeed. We can be proud of ourselves. Once in a while we indulge in a little wistful thinking: What if this person could become more of a friend, what if we could become more than friends? If that happens, we are pleased; and if it does not, we are disappointed.

Somehow taking the expectations off of new encounters opens a door to dozens of wonderful experiences with different people. This we would have missed before. This we can enjoy now.

Learning to accept people who touch our lives and then go on can be a fantastic growing experience! I now have a plaque on my wall that says, "You have touched me. I have grown." It's exciting to know that people don't have to come inside our lives to stay, in order to help us grow. Even temporary relationships can have a positive impact.

Of course we still need a few close friends who can share in the troubled times as well as in the recreational times. Those friendships still take time to grow and develop. And when one of those friends leaves us, there is a period of healthy and very normal mourning. But life is so much fuller when one learns to enjoy each of those momentary touch-and-go encounters.

It's our choice, as I realized one night after a friend had left. In my sadness, I wrote this poem.

HE'S GONE AGAIN

Before he came
  I dreamed a bit
  I cautioned myself
  I cleaned the house
      And . . . deep inside I knew each visit
      Puts a few more ghosts to sleep.
He was here
  We talked for hours
  We laughed and teased
  We touched and shared
      And . . . deep inside I responded to his growth
      And wished for his wisdom and skill.

He's gone again
I feel empty
I feel depressed
I feel alone
And . . . deep inside I know it's my choice:
To cry because he left
Or to smile because he came!

Limited Loneliness

When our lives are designed to develop close friends, casual friends, and acquaintances, we discover that the lonely times become somewhat limited. Because being alone is not necessarily being lonely—loneliness is the feeling that we are totally alone, uncared for and unworthy of love. Being alone, on the other hand, can be quite fun!

Lani, an exuberant single, says, "My family often asks how I endure all those lonely nights. They don't understand how it is at all! They must be talking about the nights I leave the dishes in the sink and watch old movies on television. Or those nights that I curl up in a ratty, oversized T-shirt to read a good book. Or those nights that I paint until 4:00 in the morning. Or those nights that I wash my hair and leave it wet while I glob funny-looking stuff on my face and relax. Or when I write, listen to music, sit and think. If those are the nights they're talking about, then I can only tell them they're my favorites, and I'm not lonely then! When I feel lonely, I call up a friend and the loneliness vanishes."

These are some of the ways to leave loneliness behind when adventuring into singlehood!

Your Loneliness

1. How much of the time do you feel lonely?
2. When do you feel the loneliest? If you can't answer this question, keep a log for the next two weeks and record your feelings.
3. List the ways in which you have ensured your own loneliness.
4. Explain how you meet new people on a regular basis.
5. Identify the people in your social network.
   a. intimate friends
   b. close friends
   c. casual friends
   d. friendly acquaintances
6. Evaluate your social network:
   Do you have at least two names in each of the categories in question 5?

Do you have too many people in any one category?

Do you have all the names in categories a and b; or do you keep everyone in either c or d?

Do you have a balance of same-sex and opposite-sex people in the categories, or do you have some categories that are mostly filled with either the same or opposite sex?

Do you have both married and single people in your network?

7. Write three things you will do this week to preclude feeling lonely.

For Further Reading

Coleman, Emily. *Making Friends with the Opposite Sex*. Los Angeles, CA: Nash Publishing, 1972.

Coleman, Emily and Betty Edwards. *Brief Encounters*. Garden City, NY: Doubleday and Co., Inc., 1979.

Spence, Inez. *Coping with Loneliness*. Grand Rapids, MI: Baker Book House, 1975.

Wallace, Joanne. *The Image of Loneliness*. Old Tappan, NJ: Revell, 1978.

5. Stretching Your Comfort Zones

Have you noticed how many people run these days? Some talk of running five or 10 miles as casually as I talk about walking to the corner and back. But they didn't just start out one day running five or 10 miles. They began slowly, ran a little farther each day, and gradually increased their endurance. Each day they "stretched" a little more until they could easily reach their goal.

Stretching can be defined as a method of improving or learning a new behavior by extending the "comfort zone" a little more each time something is attempted. In stretching you do not expect immediate comfort. You know there will be discomfort at first, but if the goal is something you really want, you choose to stretch and reach it.

A sedentary person who wants to run five miles a day will probably fail if he goes out one day and tries to run those miles. If he's foolish, he returns to his chair and says, "See, I can't do it." The wise person says, "I'll see just how far I can run. Then each day I'll run a little bit farther until I can run five miles."

"I know what you mean," Rose commented one evening. "About once a year I decide that I'm going to get back into shape, and I start up a vigorous exercise program. Of course, the first day I always overdo it, and I am so sore that I can't move that night. All I do is lie in a hot tub and moan. Then I give up exercising. But back in high school I could exercise for a full hour a day during physical education without actually being too tired."

The difference is that in high school the muscles were used to the routine—now they aren't. Any program to use our physical abilities more than we have been must be sensible; it must be built on the concept of stretching the comfort zones in small steps.

First we set a goal, then we mark the steps it will take to reach that goal. We practice and practice and practice. Only when we have mastered and are comfortable with the first step can we proceed.

"It's hard to stay at that first step sometimes." Shawn confesses. "When I first started learning to play the piano, my teacher gave me scales to practice. I wanted to play songs! It seemed forever before she would

let me play even a simple melody. First, I had to prove I could play the assigned exercises perfectly. But of course, she was right. I can see that now. If she had let me try songs before I could manipulate the keys, I would have failed—and maybe not wanted to continue my lessons."

Often our wants are far ahead of our physical comfort zones. This is good! Wanting to learn a new skill (playing a musical instrument, tennis, racquetball, or even running) is the first step in stretching our comfort zones to include that new skill.

Just as we have physical comfort zones, we also have mental, psychological, and social comfort zones. We tend to enjoy staying within the parameters of what is easy and comfortable.

However, people who are developing and growing as individuals cannot spend their lives in the safety of comfortable behaviors. In the previous chapter we discussed setting and reaching personal goals. Some people can step from the status quo and embark on a new venture using a whole new set of skills without experiencing much anxiety. Their comfort zones are easily enlarged. They are ready for new adventures and can take risks that are terrifying to others.

Other people can advance in several areas of their personal lives without any problem other than an occasional tired evening or a few small complaints. But these same people hold back in one or two areas of growth because they are too scared to move out of the comfort area.

The last group of people are so completely immobilized by their fears of risking that they do not ever venture forth into growing.

Each of us may fall into one of those categories at different times in our lives. When things are going well and we feel good about ourselves, we are often willing to try anything. At other times we are more cautious. After a serious setback (physical, mental, social, psychological, spiritual) we may feel incapable of facing anything unpredictable! And there's nothing wrong with retreating into our safe worlds for a time of healing, resting, and regrouping.

The tragedy is in trying to live there all of the time.

Planning a Stretch

Stretches must be carefully planned.
1. Take a few minutes to review your list of personal goals and identify an area that gives you a coldness in the pit of your stomach (or other signal of fear). Which one do you secretly believe that you won't ever achieve because it is too scary? (Or list a behavior you envy in others but feel you could never do. For example: making a public speech, performing for an audience, asking an acquaintance over for dinner,

getting to know a member of the opposite sex, learning a new dance, letting someone else lead in a group, voicing your ideas at a meeting, not voicing your ideas at a meeting.)

For that goal you need to use the "stretch" approach.

2. Decide that you will practice doing that behavior until you are comfortable. (Be sure to reduce the desired behavior to as many small steps as possible—don't tackle the whole activity at once!)

3. As if you were a teacher, give yourself a home or field work assignment. Write a plan to practice the first step a specific number of times (over five) within the next week.

4. Accept the following:

   You will probably feel afraid at first, even for quite a while.

   You will probably feel very uncomfortable and not too successful at first.

   You will follow through on your plan regardless of the immediate outcomes.

   Some of the outcomes will be very negative; others will be positive.

   Your commitment is to complete the assignment, *not* to get positive results. Positive results are just unexpected bonuses. Focus on the assignment and follow through.

   You will feel good about yourself because you tried.

   You will see positive results if you keep on stretching.

5. Give yourself a new assignment each week. Stay on the first step of the new behavior until you feel comfortable doing it. Then assign yourself the next step. Weekly assignments are important. If you wait too long between "stretches," you'll be starting from scratch each time.

6. Affirm yourself each time you stretch. Share your success at stretching with a friend who will reinforce your excitement.

By focusing on the assignment rather than on the outcome we minimize the fear of failure which is the most crippling fear we face. A second advantage is that we experience both positive and negative outcomes when we practice the new behaviors. We come to realize that our fears had blown the negatives all out of proportion. In reality we can cope with more than we thought we could. Stretching is a deceptively simple technique that works near miracles in our lives.

A Mental Stretch

Irene and a professor of music at the state university were dating with serious intentions of getting married. The professor, an accomplished musician who could play every instrument in the band and orchestra, seemed to know more about music than anyone else in the world! Irene was a career professional who managed her own personal employment agency and could carry on an intelligent conversation on most subjects; but she felt totally inadequate in the area of music. She had never been musical, and through a series of circumstances she had never been exposed to anything but sacred music throughout her entire life. Because the gap between her knowledge of music and her friend's knowledge of music was so enormous that it seemed uncrossable, Irene felt immobilized. She decided to stretch.

Some things were not threatening:

1. She took a beginning music appreciation course at the local community college.
2. She bought a record of each type of music and listened to music each evening, comparing sounds and her responses to each.
3. She listened to the FM classical music radio station instead of watching television one night a week and tried to identify songs or types of musical numbers.

Several steps were very scarey:

1. She decided to take piano lessons so she could more fully experience and become involved in music.
2. She shared her fears with her friend and asked him to guide her in her stretching and learning processes.

Two years later Irene looked back over her progress and couldn't believe how far she had come. "I feel as if I've stretched my brain around a lot of new concepts. I'll never be at Terrence's level, but I'm comfortable now."

A Social Stretch

Shy people, ill at ease when meeting new people, usually sit quietly at social gatherings. Or if they really want to meet people, they may gather up their courage and walk to a group of people and say, "Hi, my name is . . ." And because many people aren't always sensitive to the needs of others, they may just say hi and drop the conversation. If so, then shy people may be hurt and convinced that they have reason to be shy.

But if shy people attack the problem using the concept of stretching, one "failure" doesn't mean that all is lost. They choose the target behavior—joining in conversations at social gatherings. They say, "OK, this behavior is hard for me, and so for the next month I'll try it four times at each function I attend. I'll walk up to a group of people, and when their conversation lulls I'll introduce myself and ask the others their names. I'll ask them what they do for a living and if they're having a good time. If a longer conversation develops, it's fine. If not, I'll move around the room to another group. *I will do this four times regardless of the outcome of each individual attempt.*"

This last statement is one of the key concepts of stretching. You follow through on a program regardless of the immediate results.

Harry, a shy person, gave himself the kind of stretch I've just discussed. If he follows through on his assignment, he will eventually find that he is comfortable walking up to small groups of people at parties, introducing himself, and asking a few questions. His next stretch might be to approach four different people who are sitting alone at a party, introduce himself, ask a few questions, and maybe begin a conversation.

A Psychological Stretch

Nancy hates a confrontation. She does almost anything to avoid a disagreement with anyone. But she's also beginning to see that people take advantage of her fear of conflict to get their own ways. So Nancy is preparing to stretch psychologically.

First the easy decisions:

1. Take a class in assertive skills.
2. Read several good books on self-assertion, creative conflict, and problem solving.
3. Discuss her fears with God, a friend, a pastor or a counselor.

Then the stretch:

1. To join in social discussions at informal gatherings she attends voicing her own opinion at least once at each gathering.
2. To honestly express her preference as to where to go (or not to go) on a date for the next month.

Her next stretch might be to lovingly confront a friend whose behavior is hurtful, or to debate an issue one-on-one with a friend.

Stretching Spiritually

God is interested in having us stretch spiritually. He encourages us to step out in faith, regardless of our fears, and develop our spiritual skills. Some of us need to learn to share Christ with those with whom we come into contact. But some of us are frightened to do this.

Campus Crusade for Christ in its leadership training emphasizes that as Christians we are to share our faith, but we are to leave the results up to God.

God sometimes asks us to step out in faith and to make a commitment for full-time Christian service. He asks us to become a pastor, a missionary, a Christian educator. But more often than not, God is quietly working in the many different areas of our lives, urging us to grow and to be conformed to the image of His son, Christ Jesus.

Sometimes the focus is on trust. God wants us to entrust our lives to His care and let Him work out the overall design He has planned for us. Most of us have a few suggestions for the designer.

We know what job we want.
When we want it.
How the rest of our lives should be structured.
And we tell Him so.

Then one day we decide to trust God in one area of our lives. (Usually when we've decided that we can't work things out ourselves.) And we turn it over to God and relax—sort of a reverse stretch because we are deciding *not* to take action regardless of the consequences. But it is still a stretch. And in these times we learn the fulfillment of His promises.

"Blessed are all who take refuge in Him" (Ps. 2:11).

"But let all who take refuge in Thee rejoice, let them ever sing for joy. . . . For Thou dost bless the righteous, O Lord" (Ps. 5:11-12a).

"This God—His way is perfect; the promise of the Lord proves true; He is a Shield for all who take refuge in Him" (Ps. 18:30).

"When I am afraid, I put my trust in Thee" (Ps. 56:3).

"Trust in the Lord with all your heart, and do not rely on your own insight. In all your ways acknowledge Him, and He will make straight your paths" (Prov. 3:5-6).

And so we learn to trust, step by reluctant step. Most of us hold something back, though, not quite convinced that God will work things out the way we want Him to. Different people withhold different aspects of their lives:

Kelly has placed her job, her finances, and her love life into God's hands, but she still worries about her children.

Ivan hangs onto his career.

Vince won't let go of grudges.

Opal is afraid God has forgotten to care about giving her a neat guy to love.

As we grow and mature in our spiritual lives we learn that God's ways are often not our ways, but His ways are best. And after innumerable spiritual stretches, we become comfortable resting in the Lord and letting Him bring things to pass.

Keep Stretching

The sincere stretcher will find that progress is inevitable. The immobilizing terror which accompanies the first attempt slowly gives way to mild panic and finally is no more than a shiver of excitement coupled with anticipation.

When the behavior is comfortable, a person is ready to stretch again. He may stay in the same area or concentrate on another for a while.

Most people are growing in different areas of their lives at the same time, so they will have several stretches going at once. Stretching, like running, can be fun, even if it is hard work. You can feel yourself growing, and that is *exciting!*

GROWING

I watched a play today
of deepest love and pain.
I cried.
I hurt today.
Not for imagined characters.
but for me.

A bursting pain
tormenting my brain
into writhing twists and turns
seeking escape.
Unanswered questions
scream for help.

I breathe.
And, underneath the pain, I see
the breaking light
of relief.
Now, I know that

this pain shall also
pass.
I learned today
about me.
I stretched, and grew.

Your Stretch

1. Reread the section "Planning a Stretch" in this chapter.
2. Following the six steps, plan your own stretch and start growing.

For Further Reading

Ball, Robert R. *The I Feel Formula*. Waco, TX: Word Inc., 1977.
Claypool, John R. *Tracks of a Fellow Struggler*. Waco, TX: Word Inc., 1976.
Crodell, Frank, and Gale Gieber. *Take Ten to Grow*. Niles, IL: Argus Communications, 1978.
Wagner, Maurice E. *Put It All Together: A Guide to Developing Inner Security*. Chicago, IL: Zondervan, 1974.

6. Growing Up at Last

"We sure have changed!" commented Julie to her mother as they looked through the family photograph album at pictures taken some 15 years earlier.

"In more ways than just looks!" her mother said.

Adults do change in many ways. Growth and development are not limited to the first 18 years of life. Actually, the most exciting changes occur after one is considered an "adult." Adulthood begins with a person's 18th (or 21st) birthday and continues for the rest of one's life. And during the entire time we are in the process of *becoming*.

According to current research, particularly that of Gail Sheehy (who wrote *Passages*), there are some predictable crises of adult life inherent in the process of becoming. We can each decide that we will adjust and grow through each crisis or that we will remain "stuck" in one level and refuse to develop further. These levels are sequential and correspond roughly with certain chronological ages, but each person has his own life rhythm and will make decisions in his own time. No one develops at exactly the same time as another, for we each have our own individual growth rate.

We also never totally complete the business of each developmental stage before moving ahead to the next. This is partially due to our eagerness to take on the unknown and partly because no one stage is completely separate from the others.

As children we can't wait for that magical time when we grow up. Then we find, contrary to our expectations, that no one is ever all grown up!

As we enter a new developmental stage, we find that our perceptions change because we are viewing ourselves and our lives from a different perspective. We alter our self-image; we have an increased or decreased need for security; we place differing values on time; and we experience a sense of aliveness or stagnation.

Let's look at the stages, or developmental levels.

Breaking Free

Breaking free is the first stage of young adulthood. We want to be free of family rules and constraints. We want to make it on our own, to do things "our way." We are no longer content to be a child in our parental home. So we venture forth, usually after graduation from high school, or soon after our 18th birthday.

Leaving home physically is easier than breaking free emotionally. And at first we find ourselves torn between wanting to be free individuals and desiring the familiar comfort of belonging. Often a peer group becomes the source of this needed support.

Breaking free of our familial homes takes any of several forms. We go away to college, enter military service, travel, get our own apartments, get jobs, or get married.

Getting Settled

Once we have left home and are out in the world we tackle the problems involved in getting settled, which is the next phase. Young adults (usually in their 20s) on their own for the first time find that the external factors in their lives demand most of their attention. Responding to the expectations of family, peers, and society, they make important decisions. They choose a career, find an older adult to respect and follow, and dream about their future. During this period young adults usually marry and begin families of their own.

Yet during this period young adults have two conflicting impulses to resolve. One impulse drives them to get settled into a structure for their lives, while the other impulse challenges them to be free to explore and experiment.

Redecision

As we near our 30th birthdays, we may begin to feel somewhat uncomfortable with the careful structure we have built for our lives. The life-styles we have chosen may not fit with what we now want. Some new choices will be made. Existing commitments are altered or deepened.

As we redecide our choices, during our early 30s, we find that those parts of ourselves which were ignored before now demand attention.

Once again we feel a need to break free—this time from a structure of our own making. One response is to tear down the life we have just built. The career executive changes jobs. A nonemployed wife takes a job.

But some commitments are found to be valid, and we begin to root and to extend our new lives in these areas. We buy a home, seek promotions, and focus inward to the families we are rearing. We experience the beginnings of stability.

Last Chance Years

Between the ages of 35 and 45 most adults begin to look ahead. "My life is half over!" cries one woman. "Is this all there is?" Many adults in this stage share a feeling that this is their last chance to live, to experience, or to succeed at something.

These are the years to become more authentic than ever before. We realize that it is not from others but from within that we require permission to be ourselves.

This period can be the most difficult to endure. We face the loss of youth and physical powers, and we give up our impossible dreams in favor of reality. Sometimes we find ourselves wondering if it is worth the price to become real because the struggle often hurts. Those who, in this time of looking ahead, accept themselves and do become *real* will discover the joy of renewal that lies ahead.

Learning to be *real* with others comes after many risks, many failures, many small successes. In a children's book, *The Velveteen Rabbit*, Margery Williams says some powerful things about the process.

"'Does it hurt?' asked the Rabbit.

'Sometimes,' said the Skin Horse, for he was always truthful.

'Does it happen all at once, like being wound up,' he asked, 'or bit by bit?'

'It doesn't happen all at once,' said the Skin Horse. 'You become. It takes a long time. That's why it doesn't often happen to people who break easily, or have sharp edges, or who have to be carefully kept. Generally, by the time you are Real, most of your hair has been loved off, and your eyes drop out and you get loose in the joints and very shabby. But these things don't matter at all, because once you are Real, you can't be ugly, except to people who don't understand.'

... The Rabbit sighed. He thought it would be a long time before this magic called Real happened to him. He longed to become Real, to know what it felt like; and yet the idea of growing shabby and losing his eyes and whiskers was rather sad. He wished that he could become it without these uncomfortable things happening to him . . ."

That's very much the way it is with people. Those who are *real*—those who are open, vulnerable, forgiving, loving, touchable, genuine, non-perfect and who assume the responsibility for being who they are—can never be ugly. They are lovely, for they exhibit the character of Christ.

Renewal

Sometime about the mid-40s, a sense of stability and balance is usually achieved. If we have progressed through the earlier stages without getting stuck, we are equipped with inner strength and an excitingly rational perspective of life.

"I'm happy with where I am," commented a 43-year-old man. "I wouldn't want to be 21 and inexperienced again. There are some things one can only learn by living to be 43."

But if we reach our mid-40s and have chosen to be stuck back in one of the developmental stages, we often find new motivation and strength to forge ahead and catch up. These are years when there is increased time to explore special interests for which there wasn't enough time before: Time to grow spiritually. Time to serve others through volunteer work, home visitation, and church work. Time to enjoy life!

With renewal and revitalization comes the joy of living expressed by Robert Browning:

> Grow old along with me!
> The best is yet to be,
> The last of life, for which the first was made,
> Our times are in His hand.

Closed Doors

At each stage of our adult development we make hundreds of decisions. Sometimes decisions seem to be made for us by others. Doors are closed to us. Someone we care for walks away, or dies. We don't get the job or promotion we have prayed and worked so hard for. Circumstances prevent us from getting the house, car, or other possession we dearly want. We can't get into veterinary or medical school.

One of the most difficult situations to accept is a change in a close relationship. When a relationship threatens to come to an end, and one (or both) parties begin to feel the squeeze of a closing door, fears begin to grow. Sometimes they are irrational.

"No one will ever love me again!"
"I am worthless!"
"It's all my fault!"

When these feelings take over and begin to influence actions, the individual may fight desperately to keep the door from closing completely. All energies become focused on keeping the door open at least a crack. The total perspective is lost in the instinctive fight for "territory."

And then one day the person steps back (or is finally forced back) and the door is tightly closed—sometimes locked. Most likely it will never open again. It is over.

The healing process is often slow. We feel rejected because we are shut out of a relationship. And we reason that others do not reject something or someone good and worthwhile. Therefore it follows that we must not be good or worthwhile. But as we heal our perspective returns, and we accept the closed door as simply the end of a period of time in our life.

As we turn our lives over to God and trust in His wisdom, we soon learn that He sometimes leads us in the way He has chosen for us by closing doors in certain situations. And when we look around us, we discover that we are in a room whose walls are lined with doors. The only question is whether we will have the courage to approach and knock on other doors until a new one opens. Or will we stand still, alone, for fear that even if a new door opens, it too will later close in our faces?

In Rom. 12:1-2 we are told to give ourselves to God as living sacrifices so that we can live out His good and *perfect* will for our lives. *We need to remember—right in the middle of the pain of our loss—that God will only take away from us something that is going to harm us in some way or something that is standing in the way of His giving us something better.*

He is our Father. He loves us. He tells us:

"Ask, and it will be given you; seek, and you will find; knock, and it will be opened to you. For every one who asks receives, and he who seeks finds, and to him who knocks it will be opened. Or what man of you, if his son asks him for bread, will give him a stone? Or if he asks for a fish, will give him a serpent? If you then, who are evil, know how to give good gifts to your children, how much more will your Father who is in heaven give good things to those who ask him" (Matt. 7:7-11).

Willard, after owning his own small business, a print shop, for five years, faced the reality that he wasn't going to be able to remain solvent. Finally, after endless nights of pacing the floor making his decision, he went out of business. On the very day that he wrapped up the last legal detail he was offered a managership of a printing division of a well-known national corporation, at a fantastic salary.

Toni's broken engagement left her almost physically ill. She and Michael had dated for two years before becoming engaged six months ago. He was the man she wanted to marry; not perfect, but she loved him. A year later the Lord brought into her life the most wonderful man, far more suited to her than Michael ever was. Today they are happily married. Certainly He knows best.

People who have developed skills for coping with many changes in other areas of their lives will be better prepared to cope with changes in emotional relationships also. They will feel less stressed and defeated. Although they too will experience pain at the loss of a relationship, they will see the closing of one door not only as an end to something but also as a challenge to make new choices in their lives.

We Need Each Other

Each of us in our process of becoming needs the understanding support and acceptance of others who are struggling with problems similar to ours. Young couples experiencing the conflicts of adjusting to married life can relate to other young couples. Parents of adolescents can offer suggestions and help to each other. Single parents can constructively commiserate together.

Everyone needs some alone time. To think, to regroup, to plan, to enjoy the quiet, to commune with God. Being alone isn't all bad. But people who spend almost all of their free time alone miss the support of friendships and caring people and therefore tend to become easily depressed.

People are social beings. We really do need each other. Deprived of social interactions, few people can maintain a healthful psychological balance. We need opportunities to share discoveries, to exchange ideas, to be assistive, to receive support, to laugh together, to love, to be affirmed. A supportive social structure is considered to be one of man's most basic needs. In fact, only when a person has a satisfactory social structure is he really in a position to develop his self-esteem.

FAVORITE PERSON

Today
My empty cup filled
My need stilled
My world dehorned
My soul relaxed

Because
Your smile, bypassing words
Warmed me
Your eyes, leaving nothing unsaid
Reaffirmed me
Your sharing and understanding
Convinced me
I'm OK!

Thanks.
I might have disregarded
Conventional words
Pat answers
Theories.
Thank you for being
You.
Favorite person.

Each of us defines our social needs in our own way. Some of us are happy if we have a few very close, intimate friends. Others crave dozens of casual relationships. To some a social life consists of always "doing" something—sports, picnics, traveling. To others, a party is having a few friends over for coffee and conversation.

Developing lasting, close friendships takes a special set of skills, and people who go from one relationship to another with a very short period of time for each relationship have not learned these skills. We need to always be learning to reach out in love and to care for each other.

Christian social relationships have the added dimension of the spiritual fellowship of 1 John 1:7. Not only are we sharing together but we are also sharing with Christ.

Building a support group of peers gives strength to one's life, for even when we feel most alone, we are all truly part of the total human community. And from that community we receive feedback about who we are and how we relate. We receive affirmation of our self-image.

The task of developing a self-image is one we inherit half-done. Our self-image is built from the day we are born, from bits and pieces of praise and criticism and of successes and failures. Then one day we take a long, hard look at ourselves and ask, "Who am I?" This usually happens during adolescence. Sometimes we like what we see. Sometimes we don't. Then we begin to make changes so that we can like ourselves. However, the changes that are lasting, that do improve our self-image are usually those God makes in us as He transforms our lives by the renewing of the Holy Spirit.

Spiritual Gifts and Natural Abilities

Ever feel left out when people start discussing gifts and abilities? Sometimes wonder (silently, of course) if God left you out when He passed them out? Do you feel just average?

Well, most of us are! Most of us have some natural abilities and some seemingly natural *inabilities!* Some are obviously gifted with special abilities. Let's take a look at these abilities and gifts.

The key to using our abilities and gifts is not using the supposed lack of one gift or another as an excuse for not doing the will of God for our lives. We are to decide how God wants us to live our lives in His service and then do it through the power of God.

If we have the natural ability required to do the job, thank God for it and use it. If we do not, then ask God to give us what is needed to accomplish His will for us. If we commit our ways to Him, He has promised—

> to be ahead of us wherever He sends us (John 10:4)
> to give us the power to be successful (Joshua 1:8-9; Phil. 4:13; Acts 1:8)
> to work in and through us (Phil. 2:13)
> to be sufficient for all our weaknesses (2 Cor. 12:9)
> to supply our needs (Phil. 4:19)
> to do above and beyond all that we can ask or think (Eph. 3:20)

How great it is to know that God is faithful. We can do *all* things through Him. And that can help us have a positive self-image. But developing a positive self-image is not a one-time task! It is an ongoing process that takes a lifetime. In fact, during periods of crisis we often tend to begin doubting ourselves and losing our confidence. Then we need the affirmation of others to remember that this too shall pass.

Developing a positive self-image involves honest appraisal and self-acceptance: This is where I am; this is what I feel. Next comes the reminder, But God is not finished with me yet! It's OK to be who I am. It is in His plan. And finally, in His time, God will work positive changes in me as I yield to His guidance and continue to progress through the stages of adulthood, becoming the person He wants me to be!

Your Development

1. In which stage of adult development do you fit? (For more information, read Gail Sheehy's book *Passages.*)
2. Explain how *real* you are in relationships with other people.
3. What experiences helped you become *real?*
4. List the people (or groups) who form your supportive structure of friends.
5. List the doors that have been closed to you in the last year; list the

corresponding opportunities that opened for you because you were free to make new choices.

6. Share with a friend how you cope with the experience of having a door close in your face.
7. Do you have a negative or a positive self-image? If you feel yours is mostly negative, then discuss this with God, a close friend, a pastor, or a counselor.
8. What are your natural abilities and your spiritual gifts?

For Further Reading

Kiley, John. *Self-Rescue*. New York, NY: Fawcett, 1978.

Larson, Bruce. *The Meaning and Mystery of Being Human*. Waco, TX: Word Inc., 1977.

Larson, Bruce. *The One and Only You*. Waco, TX: Word Inc., 1974.

Nutt, Grady. *Being Me*. Nashville, TN: Broadman Press, 1971.

Osborne, Cecil. *The Art of Becoming a Whole Person*. Waco, TX: Word Inc., 1978.

Osborne, Cecil. *The Art of Understanding Yourself*. Chicago, IL: Zondervan, 1978.

Silverstein, Shel. *Giving Tree*. New York, NY: Harper and Row, 1964.

Stein, Edward. *Beyond Guilt*. Philadelphia, PA: Fortress Press, 1972.

7. Coping with Criticism

Coping with criticism is something few of us do as well as we would like to do.

Have you ever realized that we sometimes treat criticism as if it were our most prized possession? Most of us have a mental gallery where we hang each criticism worthy of note. Think back to your earliest memory of being criticized, of feeling that you didn't measure up. Remember the hurt? Can you visualize the scene, recall every detail of that moment? Most of us can.

In fact we tend to remember our collected criticisms better than we do the compliments we've received during our lives.

On our gallery walls we hang the time mom angrily said we'd never amount to anything because of some childish deed. We frame the taunts of schoolmates. The burning embarrassment of mispronouncing words in a group of adults. The negative feedback someone told us "because I thought you would want to know."

The most recent addition to my gallery happened last spring in one of my classes. We were working in small groups and getting nowhere on the assignment. I was sure I had the solution, but no one either agreed with me or had a better idea. My persuasive skills exhausted, I withdrew from the discussion to begin sketching out my ideas. Perhaps in writing they would be more persuasive.

Just then the one person in the group for whom I had a great deal of respect turned to me and said, "Are you going to join the group or just sit there and pout?"

I don't remember much from the whole semester's class, but that one moment is immortalized in my mental gallery!

So the first thing we do with criticism is to hang on to it, frame it. Keep it alive!

The second thing we do is to spend time in our galleries at the most unlikely times. Do we stop at the peak of our most successful achievement and review our gallery to maintain humility? Not usually. No, we retreat to our hurts when we are hurt anew. When we are criticized and feeling a loss of self-esteem, we virtually run to the walls and point to a similar criticism, reliving the previous pain in addition to the current one. Not a very productive approach!

71

The third thing we do (and notice that I am saying "we," for I am guilty also) is to seek out criticism. Think back to when you received your last performance report. What did your eyes single out? The three outstanding ratings? The two average marks? The nice comments at the bottom of the page? No, it's that last comment at the end of the second long paragraph that has extolled your virtues . . . the one that says, "*but* sometimes you seem to care too much and get overly involved with the problems of your clients."

"What does the boss mean?" we demand of ourselves. "How can I care 'too much'? That's what I'm supposed to do! Care!" So what if in the process we develop ulcers, headaches and anxiety attacks?

Why do we collect, relive, and look for criticism? Perhaps to get attention and sympathy. If I tell you how great someone said I was, you may not listen, or you may think that I am conceited. You may not give me the strokes I want. But if I tell you how someone unjustly criticized me, you might listen and give me some very positive strokes. Or perhaps we handle criticism in these strange ways because we have never learned how to cope with it more constructively. Remember when your first-grade "friends" called you names, and you went to mother? What did she do? She might have discounted the friends. ("They're just jealous!") Or advocated avoidance. ("Just stay inside and don't play with them for a while.") Or rewarded the pain. ("Have some cookies and milk, you'll feel better.") Or even discounted you. ("What kind of friends do you have anyway?")

Very few parents teach their children to cope with criticism. So this skill is one we acquire at some point in adulthood.

Who's Doing the Criticising?

"I respond differently to the same criticism, depending on who is doing the criticising!" Gary says.

Most of us do. Consider the following list of eight negative messages:

"You are stupid."	"You are unfriendly."
"You are a failure."	"You are a bore."
"You are incompetent."	"You are selfish."
"You are dishonest."	"You are ugly."

How would you respond if these messages came from—

your parent?	someone you don't like?
a close friend?	your child?
someone you respect?	yourself?

73

Would you respond differently in one or more of these situations? Our inner attitudes toward ourselves and others often determine our responses to others. Dr. Thomas Harris in *I'm OK—You're OK* (Harper and Row, 1969) tells us of four inner attitudes or ego states.

I'm not OK—you are OK.
I'm not OK—you are not OK.
I'm OK—you are not OK.
I'm OK—you are OK.

Let's see how we respond when we are in each of these states.

1. *I'm not OK—you are OK.* In this ego state people tend to think that they must always solicit, listen to and obey the instructions, agree with opinions, or heed the negative feedback of others. They do not have faith in their own opinions or ideas. Other people are automatically and always right. Since this ego state characterizes the person with a negative self-image, the emotional responses to receiving criticism are (typically) feeling belittled, embarrassed, put down, hurt, dependent on others, and a desire to avoid others, or opportunities for further criticism. Even when people in this ego state accept the criticism and take corrective action, the long-range effects are basically non-productive because the poor self-image has been reinforced.

2. *I'm not OK—you are not OK.* Because people in this ego state not only discount themselves but also others, they have no respect for the feedback—constructive or otherwise—from others. They view the world as full of people with ulterior motives, stupid ideas, and no intrinsic value.

   Therefore criticism from others doesn't necessarily reinforce the poor self-image, but it is definitely nonproductive because there are usually feelings of anger and hostility toward, and a lack of trust in, others.

3. *I'm OK—you are not OK.* Some people have a positive self-image. They have learned to accept themselves, but they refuse to accept others as they are. So their relationships with people tend to be condescending, egocentric, and selfish. They tend to have confidence in their own decisions and are often quite willing to be open and verbose when explaining their ideas and opinions. But their listening skills are rarely well developed because they do not value input from others. Their emotional response to being criticized is often a feeling of superiority, annoyance, hostility, and even anger.

   Consequently the criticism is nonproductive.

4. *I'm OK—you are OK.* People who accept themselves and others as

being in process and OK are in a good position to listen to and profit from negative feedback from others. It is in this ego state that people can learn to use appropriate coping skills.

Coping Skills

Let's take a look at a few coping skills.

1. *Remember that you are OK.* It is OK for you to be where you are in your development because that's where you need to be just now.

    Imagine that you are making a macrame wall hanging, and you are carefully following a pattern that is very intricate and beautiful. You are on row 19 when a friend walks in and says, "You're not doing it right! It's supposed to have beads woven into it!" Does that bother you? No, because you know that according to the pattern the beads are at row 43, and you are only on row 19.

    The same thing is true of your personal development. Remember that you are not finished yet. Yes, someday you will be perfect and above any critical comment, but that is only when your life is over and you are "finished." Meanwhile, you are only on year 21, or 35, or 56. And perfection comes at a later time.

    Another concept to keep in mind is that just as each macrame pattern is different, each person is also different because we are unique. Some patterns use beads in rows 15 and 16 while other patterns do not use beads at all. Some people take six months to get over a life crisis, while others take five years. Some people seem to shrug off rejection or accept the end of a relationship with philosophical stoicism. Others cry bitterly over what might have been. We are all OK just where we are in our development.

2. *Next, remember that other people may not recognize that you are OK.* Even when you accept yourself where you are, you will run into people who feel it is their right or duty to let you know just how imperfect you are. That's where they are in their relationships with others. Be careful to allow them to be in that space, and if you can, listen carefully to what is said. It may be something you need to hear, even from a source you'd prefer not to listen to.

3. *Give yourself permission to not accept criticism unless it is going to be beneficial to your development.* Sometimes you aren't in a good space. You couldn't cope with negative feedback if it was presented by your best friend in the most loving way. When you're late to a meeting where you are representing your boss, and you've just spilled coffee down the front of your light-colored suit, you are probably not

75

in the most receptive attitude for constructive criticism about your management style or your paperwork-control system. Or when you're struggling through a time of personal crisis, you don't usually have any energy left over to deal with negative feedback. You can cut off such criticism through a technique called "fogging."

Fogging means that you simply respond to what is being said by using one of these three statements:

1. "You are right." (If the point is correct, don't get defensive. Just agree and stop the discussion.)
2. "You could be right." (You're not saying they are right, just that there is a one-in-a-million chance that they might be right.)
3. "It may seem that way." (Not that you buy their logic, but it may seem that way to them.)

Believe it or not, responding to criticism with just these three statements (as appropriate) will effectively cut off criticism within a few minutes. However, you won't want to use fogging as your only response to criticism because giving and receiving feedback is one aspect of a relationship. If you are never open to feedback from those close to you, your relationships are probably superficial or incomplete.

4. *When you are ready to hear criticism, and it will be beneficial to your development, take time to fully discuss what is being said.* Listen to the feedback. Don't accept it indiscriminately. Remember you are hearing someone's perceptions, not necessarily the full reality. Decide how you will respond. You may agree with the point being made but not choose to concentrate on that specific area of your life at this time because other things have priority. Or you may decide to give attention to what is being said and make immediate changes. You may make a compromise. You are in charge of how you spend your energies. You make the choices for your life.

Self-Criticism

Sometimes the worst criticism we ever hear is that which we give to ourselves. We say things to ourselves we would never take from others. Sometimes when we've made some mistake we berate ourselves for a long time afterward (even years). Or perhaps during the day we blunder, and our first thought is "stupid me!" We hear a good idea and think, "Of course, why didn't I think of that? I'm so dumb!" All day long we give ourselves negative messages. Eventually we may come to believe our own thoughts! We should instead practice positive self-talk. For example:

"I can do it."
"I am capable."
"It's OK to make a mistake."
"Good for me!"
"I'm doing well!"

As we affirm ourselves, we can be encouraged and feel good about ourselves.

Singles Do Get Criticized!

Sherri (33 going on 34 and never married) tells about the typical comments to which she's had to listen:

"'Thirty-three, going on 34 and still not married! How very unusual. You seem like the marrying type. In fact, I'm surprised that you weren't married years ago. You appear to be a good specimen of American womanhood. Straight teeth, good eyes, healthy appearance, good disposition. You're college educated, well traveled, have a good job, own your own house, have varied interests.

"'Of course, on the other hand, I suppose the single life would be hard to give up. Especially at your age. No commitments. No responsibilities. You only have to answer to yourself; you can spend your money any way you want, travel, date, live as you like. Yes, I suppose marriage would be a terrible adjustment. After all, the older you get the more settled in your ways you become. Maybe you're better off not getting married. By now most of the good men have been taken and no sense getting stuck with a loser. You have too much going for you at this point. However, if you wait a few more years, you might find a nice widower. Don't you ever get lonely living alone?'

"If this sounds like gross exaggeration to you, let me take this opportunity to say that it isn't. Statements like these are a composite of just a few that I've been confronted with over the past 10 years. Not all at once or from the same source, but the underlying message is always the same: 'What's wrong, you're not married!'

"As with marriage, there are many assumptions of what being single must be like. Singleness is often viewed as a transitory state, and one is often thought of as incomplete and unsettled. It's extremely difficult not to get hooked into thinking this way yourself, even if you don't really believe it. Am I different? I don't feel any different. I think I'm pretty much like everyone else; only if this is so, why haven't I married? The truth is I'm not quite sure why I'm still single. There is no simple explanation. There are 137 different reasons, and there are no reasons, depending on what point in time you are focusing on. More important to me than why I am single is *what* I am single. It is the what that I would rather people focus on . . .

"As a single person I declared that:

> I am a human being,
>   an individual,
> I'm a mixture of
>   joy and sorrow,
>   fantasy and reality,
>   and I cherish them all.
> I am capable of
>   assuming responsibility,
>   sharing,
>   giving and taking,
>   loving and laughing and crying,
>   fearing and risking,
>   succeeding and failing
>   and making a contribution.
> I believe in commitment
>   to friends, family, intimates,
>   and ideals.
> I am an appreciator of
>   the arts,
>   nature, and
>   the inventiveness of mankind.
> I respect life and am an active participant,
>   and for that I am thankful."

Divorced people are criticized for failing at marriage. Both the divorced and widowed are criticized for being too social, or not going out enough; spending too much time with their children, or not spending enough time with them; for mourning their losses too long, or not long enough; and so on.

Singles are frequently criticized. Coping with criticism involves keeping it in perspective, accepting ourselves where we are in our development, and selecting which areas of our lives to concentrate our energies on and to grow in.

You're Going to Get It!

There is a law of nature that says that every moving thing encounters resistance. Translated into life situations this law means that if you're growing, if you're moving ahead, somewhere along the way you're going to be criticized! Since we can never please everyone, we can't avoid it. Even when we make positive life changes, some people won't like it because they are used to our old styles and don't want to get used to expecting something different from us! So if no one's said anything negative about you lately—maybe you'd better see if you are growing!

You and Criticism

1. List the "pictures" in your mental gallery of criticism.
2. Explain how you usually respond to criticism.
3. In which ego state do you feel you spend the most time? (For more information on these ego states, read any of the many good books about transactional analysis.)
4. If you need more information on coping skills take a self-assertion class or read a good book on assertive skills.
5. Evaluate your habits of self-criticism. Are you self-abusive? If so, discuss this with God, a close friend, a pastor or a counselor.

For Further Reading

Alberti, Robert E., and Michael L. Emmons. *Your Perfect Right: A Guide to Assertive Behavior*. San Luis Obispo, CA: Impact, 1978.

Augsburger, David. *Caring Enough to Confront*. Glendale, CA: Regal Books, 1973.

Baer, Jean L. *How to Be an Assertive (Not Aggressive) Woman*. New York, NY: Rawson Associates, 1976.

Bower, Gordon, and Sharon Bower. *Asserting Yourself: A Practical Guide for Positive Change*. Reading, MA: Addison-Wesley, 1976.

Fairfield, James T. G. *When You Don't Agree*. Scottdale, PA: Herald Press, 1977.

Osborn, Susan M., and Gloria G. Harris. *Assertive Training for Women*. Springfield, IL: Thomas, 1978.

Phelps, Stanlee and Nancy Austin. *The Assertive Woman*. San Luis Obispo, CA: Impact, 1975.

Smith, Manuel J. *When I Say No, I Feel Guilty*. New York, NY: Dial Press, 1975.

8. Managing Stress Effectively

"I feel stretched to my limits, I can't take another problem," Carol sighed wearily at the end of a perfectly horrible week.

"I'm at the end of my rope!" Karl announced to his son, to warn him not to ask for any major parental decisions that night.

At one time or another we each experience symptoms of stress overload, caused by having too many changes or problems within a short period or by having a few severe stressors continue for too long a period

of time. And since we live in a world of accelerating progress and change, we are all subject to increased opportunity for stress overload.

Each and every change triggers a response (i.e., a stress) in our systems. Even a change so slight as an increase or decrease in the temperature or light in a room initiates a response that is measurable with the appropriate instruments. Responses to major changes such as the emotional trauma of the death of a family member are often visible even to a casual observer.

Positive Aspects of Stress

A certain amount of stress is good for the individual. Most people freely acknowledge that they would be bored if life were characterized by sameness. There are other positive aspects of stress which include the following:

1. Personal goals—being involved and striving to reach these give a purpose to life.
2. Increased productivity—having goals that are beyond easy reach serves as a motivator to increased output, and the payoff in personal satisfaction is highly invigorating.
3. Positive self-image—developing and exercising one's personal talents helps build a positive self-image.
4. Relaxation as a reward—this is most appreciated when "earned" by a long day of hard work.
5. Flexible attitude—successfully coping with routine changes develops one's skills and helps one maintain a flexible attitude.
6. Breaks monotony—having a limited amount of stress keeps one from slipping into a rut from which escape is difficult.

Dangers of Stress

However, too much stress is dangerous to an individual. People are under stress overload when they are no longer maintaining a balance in their lives.

Few people are fully aware of the stressors in their lives. Also few people have learned to fully relax. If asked what they do for relaxation, people often list recreational activities. A third danger is that we have not truly learned to cope with stress.

One of the current theories about coping with stress is that we have a finite amount of energy at our disposal. A large proportion of this energy is required to maintain the body's physical systems, i.e., circulatory, muscular, endocrine, lymphatic, nervous, and digestive. The remaining energy is divided between physical, mental, and emotional activities. The body almost automatically distributes the energy appropriately and establishes its own homeostasis (natural balance) for normal routine.

When stress overload occurs, the balance is upset as energy is diverted from other areas to support the stress response. If the stress is short lived, the body quickly returns to homeostasis. If the stress is prolonged, sufficient energy to maintain a healthy body is no longer available and illness may occur. The physical symptoms will vary depending on an individual's inherited predisposition for disease. The more common illnesses or symptoms include insomnia, headaches, colds, flu, and allergies. Impotence, ulcers, colitis, and asthma are also related to stress overload.

Stressors Singles Face

Dr. Thomas Holmes and colleagues at the University of Washington School of Medicine developed a Social Readjustment Rating Scale (Fig. 8-1) that is widely used (especially in the Armed Forces) to determine susceptibility to disease.

The scale lists 43 life events and gives each a weighted point value. An accumulated point value of 150-199 in one year indicates a mild problem, a 37 percent chance of experiencing physical symptoms of stress overload. From 200-299 suggests a moderate problem with a 51 percent chance of experiencing a change in health. A score of over 300 is an indication of probable serious illness.

The two life events assigned the highest number of points were (1) the death of a spouse, 100 points; and (2) divorce, 73 points. If one were to list all of the other life changes occuring within 12 months of either of these events it is likely that the total score would be quite high.

For example, some of the other changes associated with the end of a marriage relationship might include:

    moving to a new home or apartment
    selling the family home
    a change in relationship to children (for the noncustodial parent)
    getting a job (or a second job)
    changing jobs
    a change in churches
    a change in social life
    a change in eating habits
    a change of financial status

These changes are significant, even taken one at a time, let alone when they are experienced concurrently with a divorce or death of a spouse. Therefore we can easily understand that the period immediately following a divorce or the death of a spouse can be one of extreme stress overload.

Another time that can be particularly stressful is when we decide to step out, break free of our prisons and stretch to grow. The many changes we make can upset our routines so much we feel that we can't quite cope. This is one of the reasons that we don't try to do a major reconstruction job on our lives. Instead, we focus on two or three areas at a time.

SOCIAL READJUSTMENT RATING SCALE

Rank	Life event	Mean value
1	Death of spouse	100
2	Divorce	73
3	Marital separation	65
4	Jail term	63
5	Death of close family member	63
6	Personal injury or illness	53
7	Marriage	50
8	Fired at work	47
9	Marital reconciliation	45
10	Retirement	45
11	Change in health of family member	44
12	Pregnancy	40
13	Sex difficulties	39
14	Gain of new family member	39
15	Business readjustment	39
16	Change in financial state	38
17	Death of close friend	37
18	Change to different line of work	36
19	Change in number of arguments with spouse	35
20	Mortgage over $10,000	31
21	Foreclosure of mortgage or loan	30
22	Change in responsibilities at work	29
23	Son or daughter leaving home	29
24	Trouble with in-laws	29
25	Outstanding personal achievement	28
26	Wife begin or stop work	26

27	Begin or end school	26
28	Change in living conditions	25
29	Revision of personal habits	24
30	Trouble with boss	23
31	Change in work hours or conditions	20
32	Change in residence	20
33	Change in schools	20
34	Change in recreation	19
35	Change in church activities	19
36	Change in social activities	18
37	Mortgage or loan less than $10,000	17
38	Change in sleeping habits	16
39	Change in number of family get-togethers	15
40	Change in eating habits	15
41	Vacation	13
42	Christmas	12
43	Minor violations of the law	11

Fig. 8-1

Stress Overload

Sometimes we accept many crises with a smile, but at other times we can't take even one more demand without its becoming that proverbial last straw. Somewhere along the way we have used up our flexibility, our coping strength, and have begun to run on reserve energy as we head straight for exhaustion. Watch for the signs that you are using up your reserve:

1. Little interruptions to the schedule or small demands become impossible obstacles. Their existence becomes a deliberate, personal attack. You *know* that the plumber didn't deliberately decide not to show up after you took the entire day off work just to wait for him. He probably had an emergency. But you *feel* that somehow you were singled out to be inconvenienced.
2. Paradoxically, while little things seem to immobilize a person running on reserve energy, major problems seem almost insignificant and are often solved.
3. Excessive irritability, fatigue, change in sleeping habits, intestinal disturbances, weight change, respiration problems, heart irregularities, depression, general dissatisfaction, inability to make decisions, apathy or loss of creativity are other early-warning signs of near exhaustion.

4. Perhaps one of the easiest ways to recognize that we are starting to operate in the danger zone is a persistent, nagging conviction that if too many more things go wrong, we won't be able to cope. Until we cross over into our reserve the question of whether or not we can cope doesn't enter our minds. We feel capable and strong.

Unfortunately, we tend to live up to the very limits of our resources. We spend all of our income so that we have to have insurance policies to cover emergencies. We schedule our time so full that we can't fit in unexpected delays or demands. And often we accept as many stressors as we can handle, not only with our normal, but also with our reserve energies. So unexpected stressors find us unable to cope effectively because there is no extra energy. Heeding these early-warning signs and intervening early decreases the likelihood of serious illnesses.

Effective Stress Management

"After next Saturday stress won't be a problem to me! I'm taking a class." Carl boasted.

It's not that easy, Carl.

Stress management skills take time to learn. Just as the stress overload built up over a period of weeks, maybe even years, taking control of internal responses to external demands is not accomplished overnight.

1. *Keep a written record.* Write down everything that triggers your stress response during a one-week period. Note the response and the time it took to "calm down" again. Rate each stressor on a scale of 1-20 (with 20 being strongest). At the end of a week add up the number of times your stress response was triggered by a stressor rated between 15 and 20. (If the number is unusually high, try to eliminate as many of these stressors as possible during the next week).
2. *Set priorities.* Select one or two stressors in your life that you want to resolve first. Give yourself permission to ignore other demands while you concentrate on these stressors. For example, give up your usual home-cooked meals two or three nights a week in favor of easy-to-prepare sandwiches or a meal at a fast-food restaurant. This could give mom or dad up to two extra hours on those days to do other things. For a short, specified period, deal only with priority demands. Don't try to do everything all of the time.
3. *Allow God's input into your priorities.* While He has promised strength for everything we do (Phil. 4:13), He also has a few other comments for us.

Setting aside 20-30 minutes a day to read God's Word and carefully contemplate what He is saying to us serves as a spiritual girding up against the stressors in life. The promises are innumerable. Try these:

"But seek first His kingdom and His righteousness, and all these things shall be yours as well" (Matt. 6:33).

"Thou dost keep him in perfect peace, whose mind is stayed on Thee" (Is. 26:3).

"He gives power to the faint, and to him who has no might He increases strength. Even youths shall faint and be weary, and young men shall fall exhausted; but they who wait for the Lord shall renew their strength, they shall mount up with wings like eagles; they shall run and not be weary, they shall walk and not faint" (Is. 40:29-31).

What a glorious promise. To have renewed strength to cope with any stressor! He is faithful.

Talk to God.

As important as listening to God's input is to us, the communication is not to be all one sided. Share with Him those hidden feelings you are afraid to voice aloud to anyone else. Tell Him your fears. He understands the pain of unjust criticism, of being forgotten, of needing love. Ask for wisdom and guidance in setting priorities in your life. With His help you can be more than a conqueror (Rom. 8:37).

BE STILL AND KNOW THAT I AM GOD

All the jumbled words
Inside my head
A carousel of
Fantasy unsaid;
All the aching hopes
Of cherished plans
Crushed by burdens of
Unjust demands,
Wind the spring too much!

Then voices silenced,
Spinning stopped
With life in focus,
Living's sought.
My body yields to
Longed-for rest.
Released, I rise
To freedom's crest,
Guided by Your touch.

4. *Use specific interventions.* Consider ways to eliminate or reduce the effect of your top-priority stressors. Ten specific interventions are given later in this chapter. Practice these techniques as appropriate. Don't expect miracles; progress one step at a time.
5. *Set up a reward system.* Whenever an intervention successfully reverses the stress response, reward yourself. The reward must be something you value and desire. For example: a new book, a new

outfit, a fishing trip, or a special meal. The reward should come from yourself, not from others, although a little praise from peers may also be reinforcing.

6. *Follow rules for good health.* The general rules of coping with stress will sound very familiar, for they are the basic guidelines given us by our parents, teachers and physicians. This is understandable because not following these rules weakens our body's ability to respond to stress, which then intensifies and results in illnesses. So we all know the basic rules, but few of us ever connected them with our anxiety problems. For review, here are the guidelines:

a. *Maintain a balanced life.* Some people don't balance work with play. They find it difficult to quit working and get involved in some activity for the sole purpose of enjoyment. Very active people who feel guilty about occasionally sitting around and doing nothing, may need to give themselves permission to learn to loaf just a little. The person who does not balance work and play does not give his body time to relax from the tensions of life. Likewise there must be a balance between roles: spouse, person, parent (for the adults), and child (for the children). Balance is also needed between mental, social, physical, and spiritual activity. Chapter 9 gives detailed ideas for living a balanced life.

b. *Get enough sleep and rest.* Most adults require about six or seven hours of sleep each night. A regular lack of sleep prevents the body from building up the required resistance to tensions and illnesses.

c. *Talk out negative feelings.* Almost every article about stress management extols the value of having a personal confidant. Expressing feelings verbally often eliminates the need to express them physically through tension and anxiety.

d. *Have regular, physical checkups.* It is important to visit your doctor for periodic checkups. Early identification of physical problems makes correcting them much easier. Keeping yourself physically fit results in a zest for living and ensures that you are in a position to handle routine stressors.

e. *Avoid self-medication.* We are a nation of self-medicated people. We take tranquilizers then we feel uptight. Pep pills when we're dragging. Sedatives when we can't sleep. And the people who do this are not the uninformed young people who are looking for thrills; they are adults, often career professionals. However, the highs and lows created by these self-medications can get a person hooked into a never-ending cycle. And the "solution," which is only temporary, turns out to be a long-term enemy and stressor itself.

f. *Maintain a healthful diet.* Review the facts of nutrition and the concepts of eating regular, well-balanced meals. Understand the roles of vitamins and minerals in keeping the body in shape to cope with unexpected tensions. Establish and follow a sensible eating plan. Avoid refined sugars and carbohydrates as much as possible; they deplete the body of the specific vitamins that are needed for coping with stress.

g. *Exercise.* There is little doubt that most people could do with more exercise in their lives. Exercise plays a role in maintaining muscle tone, in keeping the body systems functioning smoothly, and in developing the ability to control one's physical response to unexpected stress.

Obviously, none of these general rules are news to us. Yet when we understand their importance in controlling our stress responses, we gain a new desire and commitment to incorporate them into our life-styles.

Selecting Specific Interventions

Following the general principles of effective stress management helps us develop coping strength so that new stressors do not traumatize the body unnecessarily. From a position of strength we can then select the specific intervention we need to minimize our responses to individual stressors. A few of the possible interventions are presented in this section.

1. *Take a break.* Putting a few minutes between the stressor and the action required of you allows you automatic stress response under control. We are all familiar with the take-a-break technique. We stop struggling with the tax returns to watch half an hour of television. We put away a sewing project after ripping out the same seam three times. But there are other applications of this principle.

Example: Don is at work, concentrating on the report he is writing when the phone rings. He answers it, and immediately he is confronted with an angry school principal who is demanding that something be done immediately or little Pete will be expelled from third grade—forever!

Instantly Don's stress response is triggered because the endocrine system "assumes" he is under "attack." If Don is comfortable dealing with angry school principals, the stress response will quickly abate and his body will return to homeostasis within a few minutes.

However, if Don recognizes that he is getting very uptight, he may need to take a little break from the call. He makes an appropriate excuse and hangs up, promising to call back in just a few minutes.

After a few deep breaths, a glass of fruit juice, and a moment or two of relaxation, Don is ready to call the principal. During the interim his body has calmed down, responding to the lack of an "attack."

When Don initiates the call, he is in control of himself and of the situation. His body does not feel under attack, and even the hostility of the school principal will not be a significant stressor since it is anticipated and is not a surprise. Don gets the facts and negotiates an acceptable resolution to the problem.

The take-a-break technique is useful in situations in which you are unexpectedly confronted and feel unprepared for the battle.

However, avoidance is only effective as a coping technique when it is a temporary measure. You cannot successfully avoid a stressor, for very long. Sooner or later you will have to resolve the problem.

2. *Learn to relax.* Most people do not know how to relax. If asked what they do to relax, people usually respond that they play tennis, bowl, read, or have some other hobby. Yet these activities are recreation, not relaxation. Relaxation is turning off stimuli as much as possible so that both your mind and your body are at rest.

Just telling yourself to relax doesn't usually work. Relaxation of tensed muscles is a skill that requires practice. First, you relax each muscle group. Then you learn to relax several groups at the same time. Finally, you can relax the entire body at once.

Several different audiocassettes are available commercially; they guide the listener through relaxation exercises until the skill is mastered. Many colleges, health centers, and private vendors offer classes in relaxation techniques that are very helpful if you are a person who does not know how to relax.

A comparison of the physiological responses under stress conditions and in relaxation would look like this:

Physiological Response	Under Stress	In Relaxation
heart beat	increase	decrease
blood pressure	increase	decrease
respiratory rate	increase	decrease
oxygen consumption	increase	decrease
metabolism	increase	decrease
muscle tension	increase	decrease
blood flow to muscles and brain	increase	decrease
blood flow to GI tract and skin	decrease	increase
skin conductance level	increase	decrease
alpha brain waves (8-13 Hz)	decrease	increase

When developing the ability to relax, you must also develop an awareness of when to relax. Relax at the first symptoms of stress. (You do not wait to attempt total relaxation when you are all tensed up and twitching!) In this way the ability to relax becomes invaluable because it can be used in action, on the job, or at home.

3. *Use biofeedback.* Through the use of biofeedback machines you can train yourself to control your stress response, to relax, and even to control internal systems once thought to be strictly autonomous.

4. *Take a class.* If your lack of a specific skill or body of knowledge is a significant stressor in your life, take a class to correct the problem. Community colleges, universities, and adult-education programs are only a few of the institutions that offer classes, seminars, workshops, or miniconferences on almost every possible topic you could wish for. Correcting a perceived skill deficiency will alleviate the pressure you are experiencing.

5. *Limit the amount of work brought home from the office.* If you are in the habit of bringing work home every night, you are probably perpetuating the feelings of stress from the day right into the evening and through the night. Even if you decide not to do the work once you get home, there are problems because the briefcase sits there in silent mockery all evening. Very stressful.

   If you must bring your work home, then don't bring everything. Select just one or two things that can be done within a reasonable amount of time, and then you will feel good about yourself for having completed what you intended to do.

   Work in only one place in the home. It may be the study, the library, the kitchen, the den, or even the desk in the bedroom. Don't work just anywhere you happen to be sitting. Keep the work you do at home localized instead of "contaminating" the entire home with it.

   Try delegation on the job. Perhaps others can't do the job as well as you can, but they can learn.

6. *Engage in a highly reinforcing activity upon coming home from work.* Many people who never carry a briefcase home take the job home in their heads. They continue pondering the problems and issues still unsolved at the office. The best intervention for this stressor is to engage in a highly reinforcing activity for the first half hour you are home from work. This may be listening to the relaxation tapes or the stereo, watching television, reading the newspaper or a book, playing with the children, or working on a hobby. The activity must be reinforcing, pleasant, and different from work. So if you write on the job, don't go home and immediately start to work on the great American novel.

7. *Learn to make decisions and let them go.* No one makes perfect decisions all the time. However, studies show that the most successful decision makers are those who consider alternatives, make a selection, implement their decision, and then let that decision go. They do not continue to rethink the issue and wonder if they made the right decision. Most frequently there is not one right decision. Sometimes the alternatives are roughly equal. Therefore, any choice is acceptable and practical as long as people are aware of the consequences of the decision and act accordingly.

    The specific system of decision-making is not necessarily of great importance, for there are many ways to make informed decisions. What is important is that there be no redecision without new, external data.

8. *Obtain closure.* A backlog of unresolved situations, projects, or issues can be a significant stressor. Obtaining closure relieves the pressure. Schedule one day to run the errands, write the letters, clean the closets, make minor repairs, or to do whatever is nagging at you from your mental back burner. Although you will be tired that night, you will experience not only immense satisfaction but also a surge of new energy because you have relieved the pressure.

9. *Be assertive.* Being assertive means taking the responsibility for your own needs, feelings, ideas, and actions. It puts you back in control of yourself and your life. Assertive is the opposite of passive and the antithesis of aggressive. Acquiring assertive skills gives you the ability to be in charge of your stress response.

    As each person acquires assertive skills, the entire family benefits. Take time to talk with your family about the stressors you are experiencing. Invite all family members to share their perspectives of the pressures you share and their individual responses to the situation. Seek to set priorities and develop action plans as a family.

10. *Experience acceptance and forgiveness.* The images of super parent, wonder person and fantastic child will have to go. Strive for OKness. That is reachable. Accepting your own limitations and those of others makes it possible to live with stress without distress.

    Acceptance makes forgiveness possible because acknowledging that people are not perfect admits that they will make mistakes.

    Through forgiveness we experience healing of the wounds caused by our mistakes. Let us be forever willing to forgive others so that our relationships are not broken. Forgiveness from God is available for the asking (1 John 1:9). It has been earned by Christ and is available to all who believe in Him and repent of their sins. Although our family and friends may be somewhat reluctant to forgive our wrongs, they usually do when we prove our repentance through restitution. But we are not completely healed until we forgive ourselves. This means believing that God forgives us completely for Jesus' sake. Some people seem to be unable to forgive any imperfections in their own lives. We must remember that a failure to forgive ties us to an unresolved past and prevents our personal and spiritual growth. If God, the most holy and righteous judge forgives us, how can we refuse to do the same?

If you can recognize that you are experiencing extreme stress overload to the point of being incapable of extricating yourself, you may want to seek professional assistance in selecting the specific interventions that will be the most help to you.

The End of Your Rope

I walked into an office last week and the words on a poster caught my eye. "When you get to the end of your rope, tie a knot and hang on." By following the principles outlined in this chapter, you will have the strength to do just that! And more! For through effective stress management you learn to stop stress early and thus to usually avoid getting to the end of your rope in the first place.

Your Stress

1. List the major changes or problems which have occurred in your life within the last 12 months. Is the list long enough (or significant enough) to cause you stress overload?
2. Describe your typical physical response to a stressful situation.
3. How has your physical health been lately? Can you link any physical problems to increased stress?
4. How does being sure God has fully forgiven you for Jesus' sake affect your attitude toward yourself and toward others? How would this certainty serve to lower your stress and help you to manage it?
5. Start right away building the basics of stress management into your life.
6. Experiment with the specific interventions given in this chapter starting this week.

For Further Reading

Ahlem, Lloyd H. *How to Cope.* Glendale, CA: Regal Books, 1978.
Benson, Herbert. *The Relaxation Response.* New York, NY: William Morrow, 1975.

Blythe, Peter. *Stress Disease: The Growing Plague*. New York, NY: St. Martin's Press, 1973.

Brown, Barbara. *Stress and The Art of Biofeedback*. New York, NY: Harper and Row, 1977.

Page, Robert Collier. *How to Lick Executive Stress*. New York, NY: Cornerstone Library, 1977.

Schuller, Robert H. *Turning Your Stress into Strength*. Irvine, CA: Harvest House Publishers, 1978.

Selye, Hans. *The Stress of Life*. New York, NY: McGraw-Hill, 1976.

Selye, Hans. *Stress Without Distress*. Philadelphia, PA: Lippincott, 1974.

Tanner, Ogden. *Stress*. Alexandria, VA: Time-Life Books, 1976.

Wise, Robert. *Your Churning Place*. Glendale, CA: Regal Books, 1977.

Wolff, Harold George. *Stress and Disease*. Springfield, IL: Thomas, 1968.

9. Living a Balanced Life

Living a balanced life takes some planning, but in order to have healthy lives, we need balance in all areas of our schedules, so as to be more able to cope with the stressors in life.

The Workaholic

Night after night Barney (like millions of other singles) works late at the office. Often Saturdays and Sundays he puts in time on the job. When he does leave the office, he brings home a bulging briefcase of work to complete. Barney rarely takes a vacation, a coffee break, or a lunch hour. He's the first one at the office in the morning and the last to leave at night.

Why? Barney is a workaholic. He has learned that by keeping busy he has little time to be lonely, to have to decide what to do with himself, to get involved with people. To Barney, the job is rewarding. He gets a lot of strokes on the job because his work is always completed on time, thoroughly researched, and documented. And his presentations are professionally prepared.

The Parent

Monica is super-parent. All of her free time after work is spent with her children. Any purchase other than living expenses is always for the children. She spends her hours planning for weekends, so the children will have fun. When asked what she does for herself, Monica looks puzzled. "I love being with my children," she says.

We all know people whose lives are way out of balance—

Maurice is a loner.
Wally is a socializer—out every night.
Lois is so lazy she does nothing but read, day in and day out. Even the housework does not get done.
Jerry is into sports, all sports, every possible way (participating, in leagues, television watching, attending games).

Amanda is super structured; to everything there is a time, and don't be a minute late!

Heidi is totally impulsive, she refuses to plan anything.

When one area of our lives becomes overemphasized the balance is disturbed and soon our whole lives are sort of lopsided. Often we can function for years in this way because we learn to compensate in other areas of our lives. But we are not whole human beings until we acknowledge that we have many sides to our personalities, and that we should give attention to becoming well-rounded people.

Areas to Balance

"Balance" does not necessarily mean that there must be an exactly equal amount of time, attention, and energy spent on each area, but that each area receives its reasonable share.

Consider the following areas that should be kept in balance:

1. *How energy is spent.* Different professions require a focus on different kinds of energy. For example, laborers, construction workers, sports coaches expend a lot of physical energy. Instructors, managers, and accountants use mostly intellectual energy. Pastors and counselors expend a great deal of emotional energy. Yet there should be some balance achieved, so people in each of these careers require a different type of off-duty activity. The laborers need to be involved intellectually and emotionally. The accountant needs to be physically and emotionally active. And the counselor will want to do something physically or intellectually stimulating.
2. *How time is spent (alone versus with others).* Everyone needs to spend time alone, with family, with friends, with co-workers, with acquaintances, and this time should be carefully allotted.
3. *The roles fulfilled.* We must find time to be not only parents, but partners, workers, and our own persons.
4. *The types of activities we engage in.* Some of the different categories to consider include vocational, avocational, social, relaxing, educational. Each person has to evaluate his own life to see where the problems are. The next step is to set some goals, stretch the comfort zone, and get the life in balance.

Christ Set An Example

In spite of the fact that He knew He was only going to have a little over three years to fulfill His mission on earth, Christ Himself set us an example of living a balanced life.

He spent time with the multitudes.
He spent time with His friends.
He spent time with His disciples.
He spent time with His intimates from among the disciples.
He spent time alone.
He spent time with His Father.
He feasted.
He fasted.
He taught.
He worked miracles.
He traveled.
He rested.
He served.
He was served.
He shared.
He listened.
He was God's Son, the Savior, the Master, the Leader, a friend, a person.

I am sure that He took the time to admire His own handiwork: the beauty of the sunsets; the flowers of the fields; the clear, blue skies dotted with billowy clouds; for He often referred to nature when teaching His disciples spiritual truths.

Finding Time to Get in Balance

Everybody's busy these days!

Rushing around trying to accomplish all of the "to dos" they've set for themselves, hastily scratching off each item as it comes up. Hurry, Hurry. Don't stop me. Wait a minute. I can't handle any more!

Yet some people seem to accomplish an incredible amount of work. They achieve. They are full of energy. What's their secret? They must have a 36 hour day! Let's look at the situation.

An average daily schedule includes six hours of sleep, two hours for meals, 1.5 hours of driving to and from work, eight hours at the office, one hour for personal grooming, two hours of general maintenance and housekeeping details, and two hours of family interaction. That leaves only 1.5 hours for any extras. If these allocations were put into an hourly schedule it might resemble this:

AM

12:15- 6:15	sleep		6.0 hours
6:15- 6:45	grooming		.50 hours
6:45- 7:15	breakfast		.50 hours
7:15- 8:00	driving to work		.75 hours
8:00-12:00	work		4.00 hours

PM

12:00- 1:00	lunch		1.00 hours
1:00- 5:00	work		4.00 hours
5:00- 5:45	driving home from work		.75 hours
5:45- 6:15	cooking supper		.50 hours
6:15- 6:45	supper		.50 hours
6:45- 8:15	housekeeping chores		1.50 hours
8:15-10:15	family/friend time		2.00 hours
10:15-10:45	personal grooming		.50 hours
10:45-12:15	*Free Time*		1.50 hours

TOTAL   24.00 hours

Since an hour and a half a day is not very much extra time, we must be able to find some ways of juggling the schedule if we are to find additional productive time. Let's review the schedule and find ways to squeeze out a few more minutes.

On some days the six hours of sleep might be reduced to 4.5 or five hours.

Breakfast might be used as a time to develop relationships. (But remember that the developing of relationships does not mean simply being in the same room at the same time. It means that planned, conscious communication takes place.)

Driving to and from work might require less time if one is not driving during rush hour. Going in early or staying late might provide an extra half an hour. Driving can also be combined with listening to cassette tapes or dictating on a recorder.

Coffee break and lunch time can be used to make phone calls, dash off letters, run errands, catch up on reading, or other creative activity.

Cooking supper, eating it, and housekeeping chore time can be combined with developing relationships. Keep it positive.

The two hours scheduled for developing relationships is then freed up for extra creative tasks.

Other key concepts in time management include:

1. Know what you want out of life, both short-range and long-range objectives.
2. Set priorities, and do not engage in activities that do not relate to your objectives and priorities.
3. Make commitments and deadlines. Include God in the process so that your plans are consistent with His will for your life.
4. Follow through. This includes staying on schedule, meeting deadlines, and dealing with interruptions effectively.
5. Evaluate your progress from time to time, and reward yourself for achieving your objectives.
6. Master the art of relaxation.

People who are very active physically are usually aware of their needs for rest and relaxation. The body usually knows when it can't be pushed any further and demands a time of rest. On the other hand, people whose activity is mostly intellectual or emotional (e.g., administrative, teaching, learning, counseling) are not always as aware of their need for relaxation. Therefore the stress and tension build up, producing anxiety, tension headaches, back pains, upset stomachs, and any number of other physical symptoms of distress.

A Time to Play

The one area singles often neglect is finding time to play. In the grief of divorce, rejection, or death of a spouse, people sometimes feel that relaxation or recreation are luxuries for others but not for themselves. It is sometimes difficult to stop worrying about making ends meet and to find time to play. However, this is when you need a break the most. Your stress level is on overload and your coping strengths are nil. Time away can greatly improve one's "bounceability"!

To Marsha, right in the middle of a difficult divorce, taking time out to play is the last thing on her mind! But in a few months, when she has begun the reconstruction of her life, she too will need to set aside sufficient time to relax and enjoy herself.

The most common way to play is on a vacation. People seek to change their pace, their viewpoints. They seek to release tensions, have fun, learn a new skill or sport, relax, refocus ideas, revamp priority systems, regroup the inner strength, or just get ready to face the workaday world again.

In today's fast-paced world with its many demands, we sometimes do feel a need to take time out and play. People may feel harassed and want desperately to reduce the number of decisions they must make in their daily lives. Some of them aren't even aware of the signs of stress overload.

As a preventive measure to these built-up tensions, many people plan and take yearly vacations that they can look forward to for 50 weeks a year. Others never seem to take vacations and don't seem to need them. These people have learned to relax in other ways during the year. And there is an increasing number of individuals who take mini-vacations several times a year.

Types of Vacations

There are any number of vacations you can plan and take for relaxation.

1. *The super vacation.* This type of vacation is *big!* The once (or few) in a lifetime trip to Europe, Hawaii, Alaska; an African safari, or a trip around the world! The best person to help you plan this type of vacation is a reputable travel agent who can give you ideas for the best "deals" available. Be sure to check with people who have taken a similar *big* vacation to be sure that this is how you want to spend your time and money. The super vacation usually gives you the opportunity to do things on a larger scale than does a regular vacation.
2. *The work vacation.* Some people take time off from their regular jobs to work at another project such as painting the house, moving, building a sailboat, helping mom and dad with major repairs, or taking a temporary and well-paying job. An advantage to the work vacation is that just a change of pace is often relaxing in itself, with the side benefits of being productive and sometimes even monetarily profitable.
3. *The school vacation.* Do you want to learn a new subject? Or pick up a few units of credit? Then take a vacation during the summer as part of a college class. For example: camping, seeing Europe, riding rafts down the Colorado River, a desert trek, a trip to Africa. Such "intensive semesters" are offered by most colleges or universities, and this is a multipurpose way to pick up a few credits without an entire semester of evening classwork.
4. *The getting-away-from-it-all vacation.* The getting-away-from-it-all vacation can take any number of forms. Have you ever thought of going to a motel in your own city, just relaxing and pretending you're somewhere far away? Or you can go somewhere far away—to another city, state, or country.

Escaping can be just doing the opposite of your normal routine. If you are physically active, try a more passive vacation like watching television, reading books, attending concerts or lectures, or just gazing at the stars. If you are normally physically passive (cooped in an office for 10 hours a day), then you might enjoy a week of action! Plan activities such as tennis, hiking, sailing, swimming, or visiting an amusement park.

How about exchanging homes with someone from another city? Or even country?

An impromptu vacation can be fun for its spontaneity. Or savor the thought of planning one for the whole year. Will you go alone? With a friend? With or without the children? Or just take a mental vacation and spend the weekend in the backyard drinking iced tea and sunbathing?

Let's explore two types of the escape vacation.

The first is the *city vacation*, which is one of the easiest to take. It is relatively inexpensive since you play tourist in your own or a neighboring city.

If this idea doesn't sound too exciting at first, remember at least you know the language! Also you save air, sea, train, bus, taxi, and rental car fares and fees. Just think about it. What does your town have to offer a tourist? You might check with the chamber of commerce, your library, bus company, travel agent, newspaper, or local magazine. In some large cities, motels often have a rack of tourist-attraction brochures in their lobbies. It helps to list the activities that are of interest to you and your family. Borrow films from your library to show at home; attend single-adult activities hosted by other clubs and churches; take pictures of tourist attractions you may not have noticed before; ride buses and tour museums, historical sites, and other attractions in your own area. Do what you would do if you had traveled halfway around the world just to come to your city for a vacation.

A plan is very necessary to a successful home-away-from-home vacation. You may choose to stay at home, trade houses with a friend, or even rent a motel room if you wish to pamper yourself with room service and plush surroundings. But plan each day of your vacation as carefully as if you were spending a fortune on it. Don't waste a minute. You don't have to plan an activity every moment, but do get the most of what you want from the time. If you want rest, then set aside time to enjoy sleeping or simply doing nothing, but don't waste the time worrying about unfinished work or feeling guilty for being lazy. If you want activity, plan for it, then do it.

When you have your plan, all that's left to do is follow it and enjoy yourself!

The second type of escape we are exploring is the *wilderness vacation*. If you wish for the outdoors, plan a camping vacation. Take books to read; plan to walk, hike, fish, swim, write, collect rocks, or dig for arrowheads. Select your spot carefully, with your objectives in mind. You may go to the desert, a hidden lake, a mountaintop, or even stay in your own backyard.

What you do during your vacation is, of course, up to you. The important thing is that you get your life in balance. And don't forget to take time out of your busy schedule to play.

Temporarily Out of Balance

From time to time we will choose to focus on one type of activity for a temporary period of time. For example: During Little League season, the working parent who volunteers to be manager has little time left over for other things. As long as the disruption is time limited, there's no problem with living out of balance. The problem arises when people are unaware of the imbalance in their lives, and so it continues for years.

Your Balance

1. If you bought the concept of maintaining balance in your life, what changes would you have to make in your life?
2. Discuss what you have written with God, a close friend, a pastor, or a counselor.
3. Review your written personal goals to see if any of your goals will correct the imbalances in your life. If so, you already have a corrective plan. If not, develop one.
4. List the ways you have learned to play.
5. Consider your next vacation. What would you enjoy most?

For Further Reading

Apple, Virginia Gold. *A Complete New You*. Glendale, CA: Regal Books, 1978.

de Saint-Exupéry, Antoine. *The Little Prince* (tr. by Katherine Woods). New York, NY: Harcourt Brace Jovanovich, 1968.

Lembo, John. *Help Yourself*. Niles, IL: Argus Communications, 1974.

West, Bill G. *Free to Be Me*. Waco, TX: Word Inc., 1971.

Williams, Margery. *The Velveteen Rabbit*. New York, NY: Doubleday and Company, 1958.

10. Forgetting the Odds Against You

Often the odds seem against our achieving our goal. For example, do you know the odds against marriage for

a person over 40 who has never been married
an overweight person
a person who has custody of five children (all under age seven)
a successful career woman
a widow over age 60
a handicapped person
a person who has been divorced more than eight years

The odds in such situations are often overwhelmingly against the possibility of marriage—especially if one fits more than one of these categories. In an effort to be practical—and realistic—a person may sit down, evaluate all of the factors involved and come to the perfectly logical conclusion that he may never marry.

And that conclusion can be devastating to a person who sincerely longs for a spouse. Fear, leading to a mild panic can set off a behavioral chain reaction that is sometimes irrational and self-defeating.

At this point the person has the feeling of "I'm not OK. I must change—now!" These are times of exaggerated self-improvement programs, of racing to all of the "shoulds" one can think of.

The shy, quiet person joins four clubs, attends singles parties three nights a week, buys brightly colored, boldly patterned clothes, takes up sailing, skiing, and bowling, and signs up for a class in assertion training.

The hard-working, ambitious person stops working 70 hours a week, activates a full social life, devotes intense energies toward building intimate relationships, and attempts to develop a frivolous side.

There is nothing wrong with any of these activities!

But if one's attitude is "I'm not OK!" these activities are not going to ease the internal pain and loneliness. And unfortunately, if the plan works and a marriage relationship results, it may be a failure because it was formed as the result of a series of new behaviors that are not familiar or comfortable to one (or both) parties.

In God's Time

Kathy tells about her experiences:

"I remember experiencing this fear and feelings of not being OK at different times of my life. At 17, just graduating from high school, I worried about the possibility of being unmarried all of my life because I wasn't going steady then. I dated guys I could never be serious about, because if I waited for 'Mr. Wonderful' to come along, I might never find a mate. At 17 that possibility was too horrible to face. Why, it was unthinkable!

"At 19 I received a proposal from the neatest guy I knew. Gone were the fears of spinsterhood. I remember wondering if we were actually ready for marriage, but I quickly pushed away that question. I mean, one can't expect two 'Mr. Wonderfuls' to come along in a lifetime—or expect a guy to just sit back and wait until you're ready to be married!

"Nine years later when our marriage broke up, remarriage was the last thing in my mind. I wanted no more hurt. If one marriage hadn't worked—it must prove that I wasn't OK for marriage. The next couple of years I spent time developing my relationships with my children, with God, and with myself. I started to grow, to develop aspects of my personality I had neglected, and to stretch in new areas. Often the growing experiences were difficult and hurtful. But looking back after the pain, I could honestly say 'Thank you, Lord.' I began to discover I was OK after all.

"I also began to want a new love relationship. I felt confident that given another opportunity, I could succeed. Just about that time the guy I was dating decided we should talk about the future, but as we discussed marriage, he decided he wasn't ready after all. And then he turned and walked right out of my life!

"Driving home that afternoon I could scarcely see the freeway for the tears which poured down my cheeks. All of the old fears and feelings of inadequacy filled me, bursting apart the seams of my carefully nurtured identity and self-image. I felt I was back at ground zero again.

"I cried out to God. Why does no one love me? What's so wrong with me? How can someone say he loves me and wants me and then just walk away? Why should I bother to grow if no one cares? Besides what are the odds that I'll ever find someone else to love who also loves me? I'm over 30, been divorced several years, have two small children, and am 30 pounds overweight! It looked as if I were going to be alone for the rest of

my life, and I didn't want to be. I felt angry, betrayed, unloved, unlovable, hopeless, hurt, and full of self-pity!

"After a while I had no more tears and no more words to say to God. I was quiet. And in the quietness God spoke to me. 'Hey, Kiddo. You're not back at ground zero. You've made a lot of progress, but you're not ready to succeed in a relationship yet. If you were to be married today, you would fail again. That's not what you want. Trust me. I have a wonderful plan for your life. When you're ready I'll bring Mr. Wonderful into your life. Quit worrying and get back to work.'

"I felt the peace of God flowing through me, quieting my fears, panic, and loneliness. I had a job to do: Grow up. The sooner I did my job, the sooner God could bring about the relationship I wanted.

"So, I got busy. Two years later, right in the middle of my busiest day, God brought into my life the man for whom He had been preparing me. As our relationship has progressed I am excited to see how often the lessons I had only learned in those two years of waiting are so vital to our relationship. How precious is God's timing!"

When we look at the odds, our chances for happiness may be slim (whether we call happiness marriage, a good job, or a trip around the world). But when we look to God, we realize that He has a wonderful plan for our life, and when He's on our side, the odds don't count!

Caution, God at Work

Thomas tells about his experiences of trusting God with his life and seeing God work against all odds:

"I'm so used to 'Murphy's Laws,' which assure us that if anything can go wrong, it will, and any other such comforting promises, that when too many things begin to go right, I sometimes stop and wonder why!

"Take, for example, last summer. Competing against 1,800 other qualified candidates I scored high enough on an exam to be offered a terrific promotion, provided I could move 400 miles away to a new job location within 10 working days. I accepted the challenge because I had left the matter in God's hands. If this was the offer, God would just have to expedite things since making the move in such a short time seemed humanly impossible.

"How great it was to watch God at work!

"Problem 1: My house required several repairs, cleaning, and total repainting inside. His solution: Some friends (six adults, including two handymen) 'just happened' to drop by from out of state for the weekend. Naturally, they all pitched in. Result—all repairs, packing, cleaning, and painting were completed in the two-day weekend.

"Problem 2: Three other houses in my neighborhood were already for sale. Why should mine sell quickly? His solution: My house sold within 24 hours of listing.

"Problem 3: I had been teaching a college class one evening a week, and we had one more class scheduled after I was supposed to be on the new job. His solution: When I called the college I was informed that the last session was actually the 19th week of the semester, and each instructor had the option of holding class or not!

"Problem 4: After paying for house repairs and painting I didn't have any extra ready cash. Where could I stay while I found a new house to buy? (I would be reimbursed for my expenses by the new company, but only after the first 30 days on the job.) His solution: Fifteen minutes after I arrived at the house of a friend in the city I received a telephone call. 'You don't know me,' a friendly voice came over the wire, 'but the president of the company you're going to work for asked me to help you find a house. I'm in real estate.'

"Half an hour later over a cup of coffee, Mimi and I got acquainted. She took careful notes on the exact type of home I wished to buy. As she prepared to leave I told her I would have to call her when I found a motel room and give her the number where she could reach me in case she found a prospective home. 'A motel room!' she exclaimed. 'I have a better idea. I have a client who needs a house-sitter for a few weeks. The gas and electricity are on and there's a phone. It's furnished and free!'

"Problem 5: Finding the right house to buy. His solution: The perfect house, at the right price, in only one morning of shopping with Mimi.

"Problem 6: Having things work out this smoothly all of the time. His solution: In all my ways acknowledge Him, and He shall direct my paths (Prov. 3:6).

"Yes, Lord."

When All Else Fails, Read Directions

All too often we forget that we see life from a very limited perspective, and we proceed to make decisions and choices as if we knew everything. When things don't go our way, we are apt to feel frustrated and somewhat angry at the obstacle—even at God.

Last month a friend of mine bought a new microwave oven. Proudly she demonstrated it for me, obviously excited over its many capabilities. As she talked I leafed through the accompanying literature, "Do's and Don'ts When Using Your Microwave Oven." I read the instructions for use:

Do not place aluminum foil (or any other metal) in your oven.
Microwave energy may interfere with the operation of pacemakers.
Blocking the vent can damage oven.
Never use abrasive powders or pads.
Make sure door is firmly closed before using.
Pierce tightly closed containers before heating.
Do not operate the oven when it is empty.

Anyone reading these instructions understands that rules are written by manufacturers because they want consumers to get the best service possible from their new appliance. They also include rules to prevent damage to the oven or to the operator. They have nothing personal against aluminum foil, cleanser, or pacemakers; they just know that these items are not compatible with good operation of the oven.

The average consumer may not understand how aluminum foil causes the oven to malfunction; he just accepts the manufacturer's words as valid. The person who follows instructions should get long, satisfactory service from the oven. Most of us are grateful that the manufacturer has taken the trouble to protect us.

On the other hand, if my friend Cheri decides that it is her oven after all and that she has the right to use it any way she chooses, she may soon find she has virtually ruined her new appliance. And because she has violated the instructions, she would find that the company will not honor its warranty. She will have to accept responsibility and pay for repairs.

As I thought about the instructions for using the microwave oven, I suddenly realized the analogy to Biblical truths.

Long ago God "manufactured" man—a very complicated model. It soon became apparent that without instructions, no one could successfully operate, or live. So God gave some instructions—laws and rules. He didn't sit up in heaven and decide to make life difficult by giving a lot of no-noes. Nor did He make rules just to show His authority and power. Each rule had (and has) a reason. When rules are broken, human beings are not functioning at their optimum potential. They might even be damaged to a greater or lesser degree.

The Message is Love

The message has always been that *God is love,* but His rules often frustrate our desire for pleasure. We struggle and strain with the words "Thou shalt not." So the message of love has sometimes been obscured by our rebellious responses.

Several years ago scientists discovered scientific reasons for many of the hygienic and nutritional laws and regulations that God had given the Old Testament Israelites. And we 20th-century believers marveled at the love God exercised in making those rules. "Wow!" we exclaimed in amazement. And all along those poor Israelites thought He just didn't want them to enjoy certain foods, when the rules were really for their own benefit.

What about Sex?

But our insight often seems to stop there, for we don't look at God's rules for us in the same way. Today's world argues that God's rules about sex and marriage are superfluous and outdated, merely religious myths.

Some people openly defied God's laws. Living Together Arrangements (LTAs), group marriages, and communes became almost commonplace. And sure enough the sky didn't fall in. The world didn't come to an end. The people didn't die; they weren't stricken with some dread punishment. For a while the main consequences were outraged sermons about "today's new morality."

And some young Christians secretly wondered what was really wrong about pre and extramarital sex. Just why did God make the rules He did? I know I often wondered.

Then recently I had an interesting conversation with a very "together" psychologist.

"I'm puzzled about something." he confessed. "After 20 years of marriage, I was divorced. After a couple of years I helped form a commune. We carefully selected the members for our 'family.' Everyone was above average intelligence and was a working professional. We spent weeks drawing up ground rules. We agreed that people in the family could form sexual relationships—one at a time; but before starting a relationship with another member, the old relationship had to be completely broken off, amicably. The problem is, why don't our relationships work the way we planned? Why do I feel jealous and hurt because 'my girl' wants to end our relationship and start one with another guy? Somehow I don't think this commune idea is going to work for me after all."

"LTA's don't work," proclaimed *Cosmopolitan* magazine several years ago.

After a lengthy article about commune life by a young couple, the editors of a contemporary magazine that advocates complete sexual freedom stated that this couple had been lucky because, unlike most other such couples, they had not split up after their life in the commune. Instead they had moved out and set up housekeeping in their own apartment and were trying to keep their marriage together in spite of the scars and hurts communal life had given them.

More and more psychologists are beginning to take a positive stand in favor of marriage. "Whether or not to have sex outside of marriage is your choice," one noted author states, "but look at what you're choosing." In opting for less than total commitment, people get emotionally and physically hung up on someone they won't or can't marry. Or when the first passion dies they have nothing to hold them together while a new, better form of love develops. In the end what have you? Usually broken relationships with all the accompanying guilt, pain, hatred, regret, and hurt.

How interesting to discover that God's laws on relationships in marriage and sex are based on His knowledge of how a human being functions best. He knew that sex is best when love and commitment exist between two people.

The marriage vows, when taken seriously, provide the needed commitment for loving, sexual relationships. For through the sharing of physical intimacy over a period of time comes the fusing together of part of the lives of two people. His laws are loving after all!

Temptation's a Broad Issue

God's sexual laws are not the only ones which we are often tempted to break. Honesty doesn't always seem to be the best policy when you consider the short-term benefits. Forgiving a brother seventy times seven for doing wrong seems a little much! Putting others first. Bearing one another's burdens. Refraining from gossiping. Stepping out on faith. All of these do not come naturally to us. That's because we are sinful and imperfect. But once we are Christ's new people we do not live unto the flesh, but unto the Spirit.

Following the manufacturer's instructions for successful operation of an appliance makes sense. So does following God's laws for successful living.

Walking in the Spirit

Learning to stand free in the liberty of being freed from the past and to take responsibility for our lives are the first two steps toward an abundant life. The third and most important step is yielding to the Holy Spirit. For He was sent to comfort us, to guide us, and to remind us that God not only loved us so much that He sent His Son to die for us but also that He will never leave us alone again! So when we live in the Spirit, we have the advantage of God's full perspective for our lives. He isn't dependent on the odds for or against a specific event happening in our lives—He is the Almighty. Remember what the psalmist says: "Take delight in the Lord, and He will give you the desires of your heart. Commit your way to the Lord; trust in Him, and He will act" (Ps. 37:4-5).

Your Life

1. In which areas of your life are you depending on the law of averages or the odds to bring you success?
2. Describe an experience when God worked a miracle in your life against all odds.
3. Tell about a situation where you found out the hard way that God's laws were written for our benefit, and that when we don't follow instructions we get messed up.

For Further Reading

Ogilvie, Lloyd. *Let God Love You.* Waco, TX: Word Inc., 1980.

Powell, John. *The Secret of Staying in Love.* Niles, IL: Argus Communications, 1974.

Smith, Harold Ivan. *A Part of Me Is Missing.* Irvine, CA: Harvest House Publishers, 1979.

Wright, Norman and Marvin Inmon. *A Guidebook to Dating, Waiting and Choosing a Mate.* Irvine, CA: Harvest House Publishers, 1978.